ALL OF OUR STORIES

The Little Red Tarot Guidebook

BETH MAIDEN

All of Our Stories: The Little Red Tarot Guidebook

First edition, 2020.

Published by Little Red Tarot. Printed in the UK.

For all the witchy queers,

with endless love.

Contents

Foreword

My sixteen-year old self is my most effective bullshit filter. I ask myself what that angry, sceptical kid would think about whatever new venture I'm engaged in and inevitably laugh. When I first met Beth and started exploring tarot, I imagined my teenage self snorting. The roots of that projection are dug deep into a story of outsiderhood. The story has followed me into my thirties: brown, exploring my queer identity, seen too much witchy, hippy, spiritual, *woo* as unquestioningly white, middle class, and likely heterosexist. I had been pretty sure that tarot was not for me.

But as I played with my first tarot deck (one I borrowed from Beth in curiosity, and which she later gave me as a gift), I discovered that far from feeling dismissed, my stories, my teenage anger, and my full, complex self were welcomed. Tarot started to provide a space to explore these multitudes. Since then, I've found I can integrate a tarot practice with personal anti-racist work and with reflective, meditative and healing practices; I've found new depths in old relationships through connecting over tarot; I've used tarot to help me to become more intentional, and to help to challenge myself and my stories when I'm stuck. I've found it to be radical and empowering.

My teenage sceptic would no doubt have put up some pretty serious blocks to my forays into tarot had I found myself with a more traditional guide. But Beth's eldership ensured I got to know tarot through decks full of queer folks and people of colour, challenging traditional gender roles, designed with a clear eye to justice and liberation. I can just picture her laughing as I ask if it matters how I draw, or how the tarot knows I'm going to stop shuffling, or what if I picked the wrong one. She's just as interested in my intuitive and felt interpretation of a card I've drawn as she is in the vast theoretical history she holds so lightly. She has helped me trust that the deck, and the relationship I have with it, is mine. Ultimately, that relationship is with myself and my multitudes.

I can't wait to hold this book in my hands. I'm beyond happy that this light, welcoming, radical voice is stepping out into the arena at this moment of global uncertainty, change, and rapid transformation. Ready to equip those of us who don't always feel that all parts of us are welcome with gentle guidance to develop this type of authentic relationship with tarot, such that we too can step more fully into the arena.

Elena Blackmore

Machynlleth, April 2020

My Tarot Story

I received my first tarot reading when I was 26 (and, yes, kinda drunk).

Before that night, I didn't really know what tarot was – only that it was something 'annoying spiritual types' did, and that certainly didn't apply to me. This all changed when the reader (zine-writer Moe Bowstern, who was touring the UK at the time,) cast my cards at the dining table one post-pub night, laying out a series of strange, intriguing images, weaving them together and telling me a story.

A personal story, about my life.

It was totally enthralling.

Though I hadn't asked a question aloud, the cards seemed to speak directly to the situation I was grappling with at the time – one in which I wasn't sure if I was making the right choice about something, or whether I was strong enough to follow through on that decision.

As Moe read my cards and told their story – my story – I felt seen, heard, witnessed. I felt validated, reassured that my experiences were real, encouraged that I was making the right choice, and that I *could do this*, if I really believed in myself. Each picture, the way Moe described it, illustrated a part of what I was going through. I wish I had written down the reading at the time; there was so much support and inspiration there. I remember the Queen of Pentacles and her rabbit-helper, and the black cat that sits beside the Queen of Wands, described as allies on my path.

After that my friend and I were hooked, spending nights in her bedroom or mine with bottles of wine, poring over tarot spreads and Joan Bunnings' *Learning the Tarot*, fathoming out our intersecting love and community lives. Tarot felt addictive at that point; together we were learning that we were people who loved Big Talks about Big Feelings, so everything that was happening in our lives got put to the cards where we would inevitably uncover the messages we wanted to find. Tarot was fun, and indulgent, and a route to have deeper, more interesting conversations with my friend.

A while later, I was going through a rough time. I'd lost my beloved partner and my oldest and best friend (the same friend from the boozy tarot sleepovers) in one fell swoop, and I was certain that everything was my fault. I'd left my small-town home in shame. I was hiding in a relationship with a very lovely person ... who I knew wasn't right for me. My choices were steered by guilt, I was mired in untended grief. I felt at once like a victim of great injustice, and a terrible person, singularly responsible for every bad thing that had happened.

Oh. And I'd thrown out my tarot deck – because the cards had first belonged to that very same friend and I didn't want to think about her ever again.

A(nother) friend was having none of this. She gifted me a brand new Rider-Waite-Smith tarot deck. I began to use the cards to explore my feelings and process what had happened. But this wasn't the fun kind of tarot I'd done before. It wasn't addictive, indulgent, or compelling. This time it was hard. It was challenging. It was brutal at times, bringing up things I was scared to admit. And it was also soft, gentle and encouraging when I needed it to be, guiding me towards forgiveness and love. In particular, I remember realising that the Moon card showed up each time I wasn't being honest with myself, and the Ace or Two of Cups would often arrive not long after, encouraging vulnerability and emotional boldness.

The cards reflected back to me my feelings and actions and, crucially, they helped me to own them; then they showed me alternatives. I asked the cards questions, and found that they led me to positive, helpful answers – though often via uncomfortable and challenging routes. I didn't know what was going on, I just knew that it was helping me, and I was grateful.

Working with my cards over a couple of years, I slowly began to take responsibility for my own actions, I gradually learned to forgive and to let go, and – most difficult of all – to forgive myself. Tarot and journalling enabled me to get all of my thoughts and feelings out of my body and overthinking brain and onto the table in front of me so I could confront them, witness them, integrate them and in time, move on.

It was the beginning of something big for me. I began to record my tarot journey on a blog, never thinking anyone would read it. I experimented, tried out exercises in books, made up plenty of my own, explored different decks and spreads and themes within tarot. I wrote some really personal posts. I used tarot to frame moving house, falling in love, living in the Pennines, the Scottish Highlands, Manchester, and rural Wales. I matched tarot cards to songs and soap opera characters and made up stories about them. Temperance became symbolic of my struggle to find a work-life balance, the Four of Pentacles a card for prioritising self-care. The Tower became the object of my anger at social injustice and desire for revolution; the Star, collective and personal hope and belief in our vision of a fairer world.

Over time, a brilliant gang of writers joined me on the blog, sharing a huge range of perspectives on tarot and other spiritual practices. The more I journeyed with my cards, travelling alongside a diverse group of readers, the more I came to see how tarot can tell an infinite number of stories, as we each reframe and reinterpret the cards through our own experiences. My tarot writing became more political, as conversations about decolonising tarot, queering tarot, and otherwise challenging and reframing a text which is steeped in traditions of imperialism and gender normativity grew and became louder. The culture of tarot was – still is – undergoing a shift. I'm proud to have been part of it.

I opened a small shop on the side, selling tarot decks to pay the bills and the writers. I launched the Alternative Tarot Course, which has guided thousands of tarot lovers in to a deeper relationship with their cards. And Little Red Tarot grew to be a really rich and much-loved resource for alternatively-minded tarot lovers and learners. Through it I met some of the coolest people I'll ever know. And in a sense, I feel as though I came of age through that blog – living those years of my life semi-publicly, presented through a tarot lens.

Though the community blog is now retired, my love for tarot has only grown since then. My relationship with tarot is not as intense or 'addictive' as it was in the beginning – it has mellowed into a sincere and loving relationship, a slow, unending conversation. When I need to sort my head out, or when I know it's time to get honest about something, I reach for the cards and my journal. When my partner and I are having breakfast on a Sunday morning, we'll pull cards to choose a theme for the day. Friends turn up at my house looking for a reading. I still run my tarot shop with love and pride. I try hard not to collect too many decks.

One of my favourite things in the world is when a friend says they'd like to learn about tarot. I eagerly push decks on people, excited by the prospect of more people to talk tarot with. In my fantasy, tarot is a language everyone speaks, and we're all able to use it to help frame, understand and navigate our lives.

That's why, with a ton of encouragement from friends, I've finally written this book. Though I believe that, ultimately, to 'learn tarot' is to learn to tell your very own story with your cards, we all need starting points. In this book I'm sharing my own interpretations of the cards, an offering of a springboard for your own ideas. My hope is that this book will guide you into a deep, compassionate and very personal relationship with your cards – allies on your journey.

Beth Maiden

Machynlleth, spring 2020

All of Our Stories

The Little Red Tarot Guidebook

Introduction

My deepest wish is that this book is a key that opens a door through which you will step into a deeper, more personal, and more empowered relationship with your tarot cards. I do not come to you as a teacher or an expert, but as a guide, a facilitator, a mentor. In offering this book – a guide to reading the tarot – I invite you to join me in a journey. The journey you take will be uniquely yours, but it will be infused with a shared language, a common tongue: the language of tarot and its symbols.

Within the 78 cards of the tarot, we can find every human experience. All of life is here, the good, the bad, the mundane, the earth-shattering. Love and hope, inspiration and fear, transformation and completion, oppression, justice and liberation. Tarot cards show us what's really going on in our lives, helping us to see how and why we act the way we do, what works and what doesn't, and how we can create new possibilities. Tarot cards can unveil the vast and unjust systems that frame our lives, and help us imagine new and different futures for ourselves and our communities. Tarot is a tool for self-development, a device for looking in on our lives and finding symbols and images that illustrate our experiences, our journeys, our hopes and dreams.

For me, every tarot reading is a story of self-actualisation, community care and, ultimately, liberation. I come to my cards to learn more about myself, to be prompted to new perspectives, to find guidance, support, tough truths, opportunities, food for thought. When I read for others, I seek the same things. And the tarot offers this to us in spades.

The art of the tarot reader is the art of the storyteller. With these cards, we weave mythical tales that resonate with our daily lives, our lived experiences. We discover and interpret symbols, keys to the wisdom we hold inside ourselves. The stories we tell are up to each of us. Perhaps your story will be a romance; a science-fiction; a comedy; a tale of healing; a warts-and-all autobiography. However your story unfolds, whatever twists and turns it takes, your tarot cards hold up mirrors, helping you to reflect on this unique tale and claim its narrative for yourself. In this book, I offer my own approach to reading tarot and a guide to my own understanding of each card. But it is in your hands now. Your tarot deck is uniquely yours, and I cannot define it for you any more than I could define your life and its many colours and textures. Let this book be a key that opens a door for you – but let the door, and everything that lies beyond it, be your own.

Tarot Basics

If you're new to tarot, you may feel daunted or even overwhelmed by how much there is to learn. Seventy-eight cards with weird names, each with its own mystical meaning and decorated with symbols – the prospect of trying to understand and memorise all of this is no small feat.

If you're feeling that way, my advice is: don't worry, it's not like that. Tarot is not something you learn by memory (or at least, not in the intellectual sense). Feel daunted, sure – to begin a journey with tarot is no small thing, and it will change you in myriad wonderful ways. But don't let the depth and breadth of this thing put you off.

Learning the tarot is a process that happens day by day, step by small step. To begin working with the tarot is to enter into a lifelong conversation with your cards and their symbols. It is to learn a language. To begin a journey of self-discovery. To make a commitment to a new relationship, and to allow it to unfold like a friendship. As you work with your cards, you'll make discoveries about them and about yourself, discoveries that come gradually and with practice. It is impossible to get to know these cards quickly or all at once.

You'll begin as we all do, looking up card meanings in books or online, then working to apply what you find to your own readings, with varying results. Sometimes the meanings you read will seem scarily accurate. Other times you won't get it at all. Both are fine. It's all helping to shape your understanding. (And if you never stop looking up meanings in books? That's fine too. I still reach for well-worn copies of Rachel Pollack's *Seventy Eight Degrees of Wisdom*, or Oliver Pickle's *She Is Sitting in the Night*. Reflecting on what other tarot writers have to say about this card or that is one way I ensure I keep learning.)

Reading tarot cards

The purpose of a tarot reading is normally to seek answers or guidance, or to reflect more deeply on a situation we're facing. We may come to our cards with a specific question, an issue we'd like to explore, or with nothing but an open heart, ready to receive their message.

Typically, a tarot reader will shuffle the deck of cards before drawing one or more and laying them down so as to examine and 'read' them. What follows is different for everyone, but it will probably involve looking deeply into the images and symbols shown, so as to find meaning and guidance. It is a process of interpretation, and these interpretations will be different for everyone. Tarot readings enable us to lay our stories out in front of us so we can examine, interpret and reflect on what's happening. From here we can look at how we're responding to it, for sources of support or danger, and for possibilities that lie before us.

At the end of this book you'll find a selection of tarot 'spreads'. These are card layouts, where cards are laid down in specific positions, each position having its own meaning. Each card is read in it's own position (a simple example: Past, Present, Future – one card for each of these positions). After reading the cards in this way, the reader can then read the spread as a whole, finding common threads and themes, and deeper guidance. (Many people also create their own tarot spreads, deciding in advance what positions and perspectives they'd like the cards to take so that they can answer specific questions.) In that section, I also offer simple guidance for carrying out a tarot reading using a spread.

Tarot cards can also be read individually – a one-card reading is as good as any! In the next section, I'll set out a simple, daily tarot practice of drawing one card each day then sitting with that card and learning a little about it, feeling your way into it, discerning it's particular message for you on that particular day. As you do this and, eventually, draw the same card more than once, you'll see how your interpretation of the card shifts and develops, just as the circumstances and feelings of your daily life change, too.

A quick overview of the deck

Tarot is both a deck of 78 cards, and the numbered system that frames those cards, giving them a structure.

In the section of this book that works through the card meanings, I present the tarot in three sections. Briefly, these are:

The Major Arcana – 22 cards. These are the 'big' cards, the archetypes. They depict the forces at work in our lives, universal energies we can tap into. Familiar major cards might be Death, the Tower, the Fool, or the Hermit.

The Minor Arcana – 40 cards. Divided into four suits, the Ace through Ten of Pentacles, Swords, Wands and Cups describe everyday events, human behaviours, aspects of our lived experiences. Each of the four suits has a different theme, discussing a different arena of our lives – Pentacles represent our physical lives, Swords are about thought and communication, Wands deal with inspiration and creativity, Cups reveal our complex emotional lives.

The Face cards – 16 cards. Rounding out the four suits, the Pages, Knights, Kings and Queens are a cast of characters, showing us a range of qualities and skills we can work with relating to the themes of their particular suits. The Face cards are part of the Minor Arcana but have their own section in this book.

Reversed cards

'Reversed' cards are those which appear upside down in a reading. For many tarot readers, this gives rise to a whole new set of meanings.

50% (or more) of the cards in any reading might be reversed. What do you do when you see these cards? Ignore them? Struggle with them? Do you have additional interpretations for reversed cards?

Some people have a whole extra set of 78 meanings for each card when upside-down. Many tarot books will have both upright and reversed interpretations for each card. Janet Boyer has published a book with 78 new interpretations for reversed cards, whereas Bridget at Biddy Tarot provides 'upright and reversed' tarot card meanings on her popular website. Many tarot deck guidebooks present two different meanings for a card, depending on whether it appears right side up or not.

And others will simply flip the card the right way up and carry on as normal!

It's completely up to you whether you wish to read the cards this way or not – a lot of people (myself included) simply flip the cards around as they lay them down, reading all of them in the 'upright' positon.

If you do wish to read reversed cards, here are a few suggestions for how to interpret them:

- Fear of/unwillingness to work with this card's message/energy.
- Corruption of this card's message/energy.
- Blocking of/inability to achieve this card's message/energy.
- Enhancement of/too much of this card's message/energy.
- Opposite of this card's message/energy.

Using more than one deck

Before I get into this I want to say: *you do not need more than one deck.* Platforms like Instagram can make it feel as though you have to have All The Decks, and it's just not the case. Deck-collecting can be fun (I call my shop's newsletter #Decklust for a reason!) and many folks love to use multiple decks, but all you need for a deep and fulfilling tarot practice is one deck you enjoy using.

However, if you do have access to more than one deck, you'll notice that the same card can appear completely different in two different decks. Spending time reflecting on the differences and common threads is a great way to deepen your understanding of a card.

Try this with your daily card: pick one card from the first deck, then look it up in another deck, to see how the two compare. (If you don't have a second deck, you can also look cards up online and browse the many different images.)

Look for both the differences between them and the common ground they share. Think about ...

- What do they have in common? Are there symbols common to both/all cards?

- Even if the images are very different, do they have a similar vibe or 'feel'? Or is even this very different?

- What are the most striking differences?

- Do the differences feel confusing, or are the cards presenting two different perspectives on a similar situation?

- If the cards feel very different, can you 'blend' their messages to create something new?

Creating a Daily Tarot Practice

The simple ritual of pulling a tarot card every day is one of the most accessible and popular ways to engage with a tarot deck and to gain familiarity with the cards. Far more effective than memorising meanings, taking time to reflect on a single card daily is one of the most useful and enjoyable methods I know for learning tarot.

Tarot lovers of all levels of experience will draw a tarot card each day for all sort of reasons. Some draw a card in the morning, others in the evening. Some use a daily draw for guidance or suggestions about approaching their day, or processing it when it is done. Some use a daily card for journalling and exploring interpretations. Some people draw a card to meditate upon, whilst others may place a card on their altar.

Pulling single cards is a cornerstone of my self-care. When I do it daily, I deepen into this practice, and watch threads weave their way through the days of my life. I check in with myself, witness myself, the tarot mirrors subtle shifts in energy and experience that help me define my life.

Guidance for a simple daily tarot ritual:

- Grab a cuppa, your tarot cards, and your journal, if you use one. Get comfortable. Take a moment to close your eyes, take a deep breath or two, letting yourself become still and present.

- Shuffle the deck. Draw one card. This is your card for the day!

- Look at the card. Really look, notice all the little parts of it. Try to feel the card, too; try to get a sense of its energy.

If you want to go deeper into this practice, a single tarot card offers a beautifully simple framework for a daily journal. This isn't about 'getting it right', or rewriting the ideas you've read in books or online (though it's fine to work these in, if that's what comes). This is about your reaction to the cards and the ideas it sparks in your mind. Listen to your intuition as you study the card, and let the words flow.

A few prompts for your journal:

- What is the first thing you notice about this card?

- Do any parts of the image jump out at you?

- Are these figurative (pictures of people and things), or are they symbols?

- What about the use of colour? Does this feel significant?

- Is there anything interesting happening in the background?

- Which of the four elements (earth, air, fire or water) seem to be represented here?

- How does this card make you feel?

- Can you think of an event, a situation, or a person that this card might represent?

- Do you like this card? Why/why not?

- What would the opposite of this card feel like?

- How can you use this card's energy today?

You might keep your card with you for the day. Tuck it into your journal or wallet, or take a photo of the card on your phone.

Tarot for Self-Care

Through working with our cards we are pushed to get really honest with ourselves, to witness and name the forces that bear down on us, and the behaviours and habits we might celebrate or work to overcome. A regular tarot practice is a practice of getting real. Really real. Sometimes scary real. Tarot can take us to dark and difficult places, and it can shine lights on parts of ourselves we're not yet ready to love. It can highlight potential we refuse to see, or bring up stories from our past we'd prefer to keep buried.

This work can be uncomfortable. Or tedious. Or triggering. Or just really damn tough. And it's crucial that alongside the work with our cards, we bring compassionate, nurturing elements to our practice – particularly if we are working with trauma. Often, it is a profound act of self-care to go to those scary places and work through them, and tarot can be used for processing trauma. But it's important we create conditions that help us feel safe and held as we do so. Just as a good therapist puts energy into creating a safe space for their client, in tarot we are our own therapists and we need to create those safe spaces for ourselves.

How do we do this? Again, it's deeply personal. Below I've offered a few ideas to consider, but this is not intended as an exhaustive to-do list. Please be aware that I am not a trained therapist, nor an expert in trauma. My aim is to get you thinking about what works for you – you may do some, all, or none of these things as you build a practice that is nourishing and nurturing and, crucially, *safe* for you.

Developing a nurturing practice

Creating space for tarot

A tarot reading can happen anywhere – in bed, on the floor of a nightclub, on a train, on the beach. I'm a fan of getting out the cards whenever it feels right, never mind whether I have the 'perfect set-up'. That said, when possible, it's a pleasure to put time and care into setting up so that I can really be with the cards I draw and my responses to them. I recommend creating a regular practice of reading for yourself and taking the time to set the mood first – think of it as a luxurious (yet free!) therapy session, and create dedicated, conscious space where you can be present and really sink into the reading.

Here's my guidance for creating the perfect space for a reading:

- Choose a space where you feel safe, have a little room and can sit comfortably. A desk or coffee table are ideal – take the time to clear this space before you begin.

- Want to read on your bed? Shake or smooth out your covers and put away any other 'stuff' that's lying around first.

- Where will your tarot deck/s and your journal live? Consider saving a shelf space or similar close to your reading spot.

- It's a pleasure to decorate our tarot reading spaces. Perhaps you have a reading cloth you can spread out, a special candle that you light, or crystals or other items that you like to keep close by. Gather these together with your cards to create your own personal reading kit.

Journalling

For me, tarot and writing go hand in hand. As I uncover new layers in the cards or are prodded and pushed by my cards, I love to keep a record of the lessons I'm learning and the feelings I'm feeling. I'm not alone – tarot journalling is hugely popular, evidenced by the vast community of tarot bloggers online, and those who journal on social media (Marianne at Two Sides Tarot has posted a daily card on Instagram for years).

Through journalling we build a tangible body of wisdom we can look back on. Journalling doubles down on our ability to witness ourselves through the tarot. Through the simple act of pausing and reflecting we allow ourselves to sink deeper into the messages and lessons we're receiving, deeper into an authentic relationship with our selves. I encourage anyone to keep a tarot journal and to give themselves the gift of that reflective journalling time.

Your journal might have:

- Space for daily cards and reflections.
- Records of whole readings.
- A reference section where you build a collection of notes about all of the cards in order.
- Notes on cards that are coming up a lot for you.
- Tarot learning exercises (my eight-week Alternative Tarot Course) is filled with these.

- Drawings of cards.

- Letters to yourself, or others.

- Anything else!

A journal might be a notebook, a diary, a pinboard, a blog. Whatever it is, craft it with love and understand that this is a deeply creative act.

Meditation, grounding and prayer

What would it be like to close your eyes, breathe, and say a few carefully chosen words before picking up your cards? Many folks practice some form of grounding before they read tarot, preparing themselves and calming the mind and body. I do sometimes, but not always, and I find that it's a valuable practice that creates the psychic space I need for a really deep, special reading. You might write yourself a little prayer of self-love, or invoke a beloved deity, take three deep breaths, or hit play on a favourite grounding meditation before you pick up your cards. Experiment with this, see what feels good for you.

Finding supportive allies in the tarot

Sometimes, I come to the tarot with the intention of choosing a specific card, and often this is because I'm seeking an ally – a source of support. Allies are cards that don't necessarily represent who *we* want to be ourselves, but the people or energies we need around us, the kinds of support or encouragement or practical help we might look for. This is a chance to really think about you needs (including, or perhaps especially, the kinds of help you may be too afraid to ask for).

Look through your deck and pull out one or two cards you'd like as your allies. Note the qualities represented in these cards. What kinds of people would your best allies be? What kinds of things would they do that would be helpful to you? Going further, you can look at finding these qualities in real life. Do you have these people around you? Where could you go, or what could you be part of, where you might find this kind of support?

Creating an altar

Creating an altar can be a really beautiful way to round out a reading and bear witness to the most profound messages you received. This has been a part of my own tarot practice for years. An altar is simply a consciously dedicated space – and it can be dedicated to whatever we like. My altars focus on energies or ideas I want to celebrate or welcome into my life. I may pull out the key card or cards from a reading, or consciously choose cards from my deck, using these as the centrepiece of an altar. I decorate altars with symbolic objects, everyday items codified to represent other elements of the energies and ideas I'm working with.

Here's my process for creating an altar:

I usually choose a night when I'm alone. I tidy my living space, clean down my altar, light a candle and take some grounding breaths.

- Begin with a little journalling. What are you honouring with this altar? Possible ideas could be a change or shift that's happening in your life or that you want to bring about, an intention you want to set, or something you'd like to give gratitude for or celebrate. Take some time to feel into what this altar is all about, make notes in your journal.

- Choose cards to represent this moment, intention or feeling. You can choose one, two, three or more cards. Really take some time over this – it's a lovely opportunity to look for really special allies in your tarot deck.

- Do you want to add any other symbolic objects to your altar? You might wander around your house or go for a walk and see what you find. Listen for objects calling to you, suggesting themselves. The art of altar creation is so much about codifying objects – anything can mean anything, if it means it to you!

- Do you want to create anything for the altar? A painting, a poem, a sketch, a sculpture?

- Do you feel you want to decorate your altar any further? Not everything has to be symbolic – altars are also visual art and expressions of your creativity. You might think about cloths, flowers, shells – whatever catches your eye or feels good.

The Alternative Tarot Course offers a full chapter delving into nurturing spiritual practices, including altar creation, reframing cards, crafting your own tarot spreads and reading with the moon. Visit littleredtarot.com/atc for more information.

Keeping safe

Removing triggering cards from your deck

Maybe there's a card in your deck that is so deeply associated with a person or experience that you really don't feel safe when you see it. My advice? Remove the card from your deck. You get to decide what your tarot deck feels like. There are no bosses in tarot, there's no 'wrong way', and if you want to customise your deck so that it feels safe for you, go for it. Keep it safe so you can bring it back in at a future time, chuck it in the bin, ask a friend to keep it for you, or ritually burn and release the card (along with whatever it represents).

Reading with or calling a friend

Tarot has opened space for some of the most profound conversations I've ever had with my friends. Though this book is focused on reading for ourselves and creating a personal practice, it can be immensely reassuring and helpful to have a loved one beside us as we come to our cards, reading for and with each other can be a beautiful way to deepen a friendship. If a friend isn't available to be with you, you might want to call a friend after your reading to discuss what came up for you – especially if your reading led you to confront traumatic memories or left you feeling unsafe.

A note on trauma and therapy

Tarot reader and activist Leah Lakshmi Piepzna-Samarasinha once told me that tarot was an accessible form of therapy available to her after she left home and moved to New York City with no money and a lot of shit to process. This remains one of the key drivers in my work to share tarot and encourage folks to use it for growth and empowerment – once you have a deck, its gifts and wisdom are infinitely free.

However, if you know you are wanting to process trauma or PTSD, and you are not sure that you will be able to keep yourself safe, and if therapy is accessible to you, consider seeing a professional therapist alongside developing a tarot practice. I say this not least as a disclaimer – I am not a therapist, nor am I able to write with authority on the effects of serious trauma on our lives. I want you to be safe and well, even as you do the challenging work of self tarot reading. I am inspired by folks who have used tarot to bring forth themes and experiences which they then take and explore further with an experienced therapist.

Queering and Liberating Tarot

In the global west, where I and much of my tarot community are based, mainstream culture is defined by capitalism, patriarchy and white supremacy, pushing those who don't conform to the margins. Our culture is heteronormative and cisnormative, and centres physical ideals that are far from the realms of possibility and/or desire for many. Capitalism and its cultural foot soldiers work tirelessly and violently to instil in us a sense that we are not enough, or too much, or both. A sense that we are broken, imperfect, incorrect. A sense that we do not belong.

Tarot is a tool of self-actualisation and community liberation, of self and community care. As such, a personal tarot practice must undermine society's harmful messages – so that we can each uncover and work with the fabulous, diverse qualities that make us who we are; so that we can bring our whole selves and our gifts into being.

Unfortunately, much of society's oppressive structure is reflected in the traditional tarot deck. The Face cards are historically known as the 'court' – they form royal families that head up four 'realms'. The Hierophant is most often represented as a pope-like figure in robes, surrounded by the riches of the (white) Christian church. In the majority of tarot decks, every single character is white, slim, able-bodied. The Lovers are heterosexual, and two. The Empress is a maternal, feminine ideal; her counterpart the Emperor a strong, 'manly' man. Abundance is presented as material wealth.

Unless we work to deconstruct them, our tarot cards can reflect back a limited and oppressive world view. If we are to re-imagine society and use tarot for liberatory purposes, we need to tell new stories with our cards and use them to help us imagine new possibilities and different futures for ourselves and our communities.

My approach to tarot – the approach I encourage in this book – is rooted in subjective interpretation. How can it not be? There is no objectivity in tarot – even in the Justice card. Each of us responds to the cards from our unique position in life, positions shaped by our very different lived experiences, informing very different world views. From our demographics to our childhood experiences, our schooling to our age, our systemic privileges and oppressions to our particular personalities, no two readers will interpret a tarot card in quite the same way.

This is why we need so very many decks, and so many books, so many teachers and bloggers, so many readers. We need queer tarot decks, Black tarot decks and decks that centre people of colour, trans tarot decks, genderqueer decks, decks that centre fat bodies and disabled bodies and other non-conforming bodies, sex worker decks, decks that celebrate the many different ways we have relationships, decks that reject the traditional hierarchical and imperial framework. We need tarot decks that are created specifically by and for these 'non-normative' communities, and decks that are inclusive of all and more.

As I write this in 2020, there is a beautiful and growing selection of diverse decks on offer, and a growing conversation around the importance of these decks as tools for personal and collective liberation. As the owner of a small, independent tarot store, I'm proud to stock many of these harder-to-find decks, whilst others are widely available. A few I'd love to highlight include:

- **The Numinous Tarot, by Cedar McCloud.** This colourful, encouraging deck features a wonderfully diverse cast of characters. Many cards have been renamed, and the guidebook uses gender-neutral language throughout.

- **The Melanated Classic Tarot, by Oubria Tronshaw.** This revolutionary deck recreates the traditional Rider-Waite-Smith tarot with entirely Black and brown characters.

- **Dust II Onyx Tarot, by Courtney Alexander.** This sumptuous deck is rooted in Black culture, icons, myths and symbolism, rendered in rich oil paintings and accompanied by a detailed guidebook.

- **The Next World Tarot, by Cristy C Road.** This large tarot deck places anti-capitalist punk counterculture at its core – it is a work of science fiction, presenting a post-revolutionary world of gorgeous chaos and diversity. It's brilliantly colourful, brash and radical, and its guidebook pushes readers to to root our spiritual practice fearlessly and firmly in collective liberation.

- **Thea's Tarot, by Ruth West.** Created in the 80s as a second-wave feminist, lesbian deck, Thea's Tarot was recently republished by Metonymy Press, along with a new guidebook, *She Is Sitting in the Night*, by Oliver Pickle. This book repositions the deck as a queer, DIY, liberatory. Thea's Tarot, used alongside the book, is my personal favourite.

There are many others. For a list of diverse decks, along with reviews, interviews and more, I recommend Asali's Tarot of the QTPOC project, found at asaliearthwork.com/tarot-of-the-qtpoc, and AMJ's Brown Girl Tarot Library, at browngirltarot.com/library.

In a recent customer survey, South Asian and Indigenous respondents shared their dismay at the lack of tarot decks for brown people, and the way Indigenous peoples are frequently reduced to insulting stereotypes. And as many have noted, at this time there is still a dearth of progress around body inclusivity in tarot. In particular the representation of disabled/differently-abled bodies and fat bodies — where present at all — is so often clichéd or reductive. Whilst our tarot collections slowly become more inclusive and we celebrate each new creation from the margins, it's clear there there is still a long way to go.

For these reasons and more, still many of us do not feel we have found 'the perfect deck' — the one that truly mirrors our own lived experiences, our aspirations and our fears. Furthermore, with an increasingly gentrified 'spirituality market', alongside the fact that many of these diverse decks are self-published and thus cost twice as much as mass-market decks, many of us are priced out of the quest for the 'perfect deck'.

This is where we may call on our personal power: the indomitable power of the reader who makes the tarot their own. Yes, it's an amazing and validating feeling to find ourselves and our communities reflected in our cards, and the creation and proliferation of these decks is vital and important part of our collective movement towards a more liberated, inclusive society. At the same time, don't forget, it's what you do with it that counts. It's the way we read our cards, our approach to the tarot as a whole, that will allow us to make it personal and use our cards for our own empowerment and liberation. Whilst Thea's Tarot is my favourite, I can still pick up my old Rider-Waite-Smith deck and give myself a fully liberated, queer-as-hell reading. The images on your cards are important, but they are not the end of the story — even your most beloved deck is still somebody else's creation. In your hands, it becomes something different. A new story begins — one that only you can tell. We, as readers from a wide range of backgrounds, get to filter those symbolic images through our own experiences, using them to tell our own stories and the stories of our communities. It's a beautiful kind of spiritual science fiction, reimagining old tropes in vital new ways. For me, this is a huge part of tarot's inherent magic. Though this book sets out my own interpretations of the cards, as I've said and will always maintain, these are not end points to be memorised and regurgitated. They are suggestions, jumping-off points to help inspire and encourage your own personal interpretations.

A Card-by-Card Guide to the Tarot

As I've said, the card interpretations offered in this section are not end points. I've seen the same card mean a hundred different things in as many different readings. What I present here is an attempt to summarise some of those many, many interpretations into an accessible form. Please know that there is no definitive guide to the tarot and no book that can tell you 'what the cards truly mean'. That work is yours and yours alone.

In offering this guide, I invite you to slowly, over time, craft your own set of card meanings. When you look up cards in this book, take my words as suggestions, possibilities, jumping-off points. If you get a totally different message to the one I offer, then let yours be the 'right' one. Please feel absolutely free to scribble all over these pages, gradually overwriting my ideas with your own.

These interpretations are the distillation of many years of working with my cards and are informed, of course, by the unique position I hold in this big, diverse world. I am a white, queer, cis, middle class, able-bodied woman. My body more or less conforms to the 'standard' beauty norm. I live in the UK. I had an easy childhood. So whilst these card interpretations are intended to be accessible to and inclusive of all, I invite you to return regularly to the previous section on queering and liberating the tarot. The most important and 'true' meanings of the cards are the ones that tell *your* story. My hope is that this guide can offer some inspiration for that very personal project.

I also want to say that today, tomorrow, or on any other day, I could sit down and re-write this guide... and turn out 78 wholly different card interpretations. For the sake of getting something down, I have committed these ideas to paper, but they do not, and cannot, represent the totality of my thinking and feeling on any particular card. The work of interpreting and reinterpreting the cards is a continually unfolding practice in my life, as I hope it will be in yours.

A note on card titles

For clarity and accessibility, I've stuck with the standard names of the cards. By 'standard' I mean those used in the Rider-Waite-Smith Tarot, and thus the vast majority of decks and other tarot books, courses and websites.

A growing number of decks rename their cards for various reasons - often as a way of decolonising, queering or otherwise reclaiming the tarot. The same is true of the Minor Arcana's suits, and of the Face cards (also known as the court cards), which we'll come to later.

If your deck has different card titles and you find this confusing, I recommend writing your own card names right into this book, so you can refer to them with ease.

The entire contents of this card-by-card guide are also available for free at littleredtarot.com/library.

The Major Arcana

The tarot is comprised of two parts: the 22 cards of the Major Arcana, and the 56 cards of the Minor Arcana.

The Minor Arcana (which we'll explore in the nest section) is concerned with the smaller, day-to-day elements of our lives – relationships, experiences, the details that make up the bigger picture.

The Major Arcana, however, is about that 'big' picture.

These cards show us universal experiences, archetypes of the powers that influence all of our lives, such as love, hope, manifestation of great ideas, revolution, fear, loneliness, desire, tradition, society, nature … and more. (Such themes are present in the Minor Arcana, too, but are shown in a more down-to-earth, everyday way.)

The Fractal nature of the Major Arcana

What we practice at the small scale sets the pattern for the whole system.[1]

I came across the concept of 'fractals' via adrienne maree brown's 2017 book, *Emergent Strategy*. She writes of the echoing outwards — and back inwards — of everything we practice, that 'how we are at the small scale is how we are at the large scale.' The way we act in our everyday lives sets the culture and the structure for our society. And vice versa: we reflect in our daily lives the practices modelled to us by our communities, our societies. This empowering (and possibly overwhelming) reality shows up in the Major Arcana and can help us understand archetypes.

When faced with these 'big' cards, we are asked to look at patterns, structures, cultures and systems that we are part of, and to own our participation in these. The archetypes of the Major Arcana are not disembodied 'universal themes', but powerful mirrors of culture and behaviour that can be grasped and worked with and *used*. When you explore the cards in this section, imagine 'fractalising' their energies downwards, seeking to recognise the daily practices that you engage in that help to create that wider culture, and how that culture shapes you in turn. In particular cards that explicitly deal with ethics (the Lovers, Justice, the Wheel of Fortune and others) are aided by this framework. Understand that these cards reflect the potential of your own actions, and that whilst they themselves seem huge, that hugeness is a mirror to your own power to shape change.

The Fool's journey

The 22 cards of the Major Arcana are numbered 0-21. We begin with card zero, the Fool: a blank canvas. We end with card 21, the World: completion. In-between, all kinds of strange, wonderful and terrible things take place. The

---

[1] adrienne maree brown, *Emergent Strategy: Shaping Change, Changing Worlds*, 2017.

final card – the World – completes a cycle and leads us perfectly back to zero, where we begin again as the Fool.

'The Fool's journey' is a term often used to describe the way the Major Arcana tells a story. We meet the Fool first of all, at zero; nothing. We then follow this character on an intriguing journey much like the sort a hero might follow in myths and legends. There is learning, there is falling. There are choices, there are mistakes. There is spirituality, and materialism. There are great moments of clarity ... and periods of destruction and loss. And, ultimately, we reach the end – the World – and the journey is complete, the lessons integrated.

Exploring the Major Arcana

Many tarot writers talk about the Major Arcana as being divisible into parts, each with their own theme or way of relating to the journey of the first card, the Fool. Notably, Rachel Pollack sees the Major Arcana as three sequences of equal length. In her classic text, *Seventy Eight Degrees of Wisdom*, Pollack sets the Fool aside, then lays out the other 21 cards in three rows of seven. She explores cards 1-7 as 'The Worldly Sequence' in which we see a 'process of maturity' from dependant child to a fully independent persona. Cards 8-14 then see this persona 'turn inwards', where it grapples with 'the challenges of the inner self'. Finally, cards 15-21 depict a greater journey where the persona moves towards enlightenment and the ultimate fulfilment we find in the last Major card, the World.

Laying out the cards in these three lines and exploring them in this way provides a valuable framework for understanding the Fool's Journey. I encourage any tarot learner to experiment with this in order to deepen their understanding of the tarot as a vast text, in which everything is related (we do a lot of this in the Alternative Tarot Course). Uncovering layers, intersections, common themes and distinct sequences and groups within the tarot helps us to break down and unpack its immense universe of archetypes. This kind of work also allows us to take a more scholarly approach to the tarot, offering frameworks that help us to see the traditional narratives that run through the cards and relate them to established psycho/spiritual systems such as Jungianism, the classic 'Hero's journey', and so on. And it is often helpful to think about the cards in sequence, as a progression, with each card a part of a bigger journey. This is something we experiment with a lot in The Alternative Tarot Course.

Though I have played with this approach and many others and found them helpful and illuminating, ultimately my understanding of the Major Arcana does not rest on such forms. When we read tarot, we repeatedly and routinely disrupt this sequence through shuffling. I see the Major Arcana as I do the entire tarot – as one unified whole, composed of individual cards. By its shuffle-able, apparently random nature, tarot offers its cards in near-infinitely variable order. The many parts make up the whole, and, just as in my messy life, moments come in their own sequences – rarely are these numerical or even logical. Instead the thread that runs them together is chaotic and as unique as my own life story.

One day I may draw the Empress and relate to the creative, life-affirming properties of this almighty femme. The following day I may draw Death, and be inspired to witness and honour the changes that are taking place in my life. The next, I may draw the Wheel of Fortune, and be prompted to examine the parts of my life where I feel in or out of control. A scholarly approach is enjoyable when I set aside time to really study tarot; but it's not how I come to the tarot in my daily life, seeking guidance, inspiration, or a good kick up the ass.

For the purpose of this book, which is focused on tarot's application in shaping our personal stories, I present the Major Arcana in linear, numerical order, but I do not divide the 22 cards into further sections. As mentioned in the section on Tarot for Self-Care), I encourage you to keep a journal of the cards you draw each day, and to notice the twisting, turning path that links them through time, and through the passing of days. This sequence won't be numerical, it won't reflect the 'correct order' of the cards; nevertheless, it will be a perfect sequence, because it is uniquely yours.

What is an 'archetype'?

> *The twenty-two cards of the Major Arcana depict the great myths that we personally lead. [... These cards may represent] pivotal persons who have influenced us, as well as situations, lessons, conflicts, choices, and blessings that have shaped the course of our lives. Through their role in the Tarot, the Major Arcana offers us the opportunity to reflect on these points and embrace them as the great mythic stories that they are.*
>
> *Courtney Weber,* Tarot for One

When we talk about 'archetypes' in the Major Arcana, we are referring to recognisable motifs, a representation of a 'type' that we recognise and understand. They offer us a way of understanding complex concepts via a familiar form.

The Major Arcana is made up of such archetypes – some more familiar than others. The Hermit is a good example: a hooded figure, bearded, leaning on his staff, living alone atop a mountain or at the edge of the forest. Death is another: the grim reaper, skeletal, cloaked in black, coming for us all with her scythe, reminding us of our own mortality and that all things end (or rather, change). Or what about the High Priestess: a mysterious, silent figure who operates from pure intuition, and holds the key to the collective unconscious? How about the Chariot (a driven, determined hero), the Emperor (the strict ruler) or the Empress ('mother nature')?

These archetypes are often found in books or films, drawn from mythologies. Our exposure to popular culture (along with the fact that we carry the stories of our ancestors within us) means we recognise most of them, though we may not always know from where. They are representations of a thing, rather than the thing itself. They are whatever they represent to you – your response may be one of love and respect, or disgust and fear. This is why one person may say, 'Oh, I love the Tower card, it shakes things up!', whereas another may say, 'Ugh, I *hate* that card. Last time I saw it, it was like the rug had been pulled from under me.' Or why the Hierophant might represent a beloved spiritual teacher to one person, whereas to another it is a reminder of an oppressive religious upbringing.

For each card in this section, I first introduce the card as an archetype. What does it represent, what are its themes and symbols? What is this card all about?

I then go on to discuss 'advice' from that card. This is to offer a more practical interpretation of the card's meaning – beyond what it represents as an archetype, what might it actually mean in a tarot reading? What might it be telling you, encouraging, or advising?

After this, I have listed a few key ideas to summarise the card, and, lastly, some common symbols often found on this card.

Archetypal representations of binary gender

In all cases, I have sought to detach the card from its traditional 'gender', and I use a mixture of gender pronouns interchangeably throughout this guidebook. For me the consistent association of (for example) the Empress with femininity is problematic, as it reinforces widely held beliefs that women and femmes are naturally caring, giving, etc. The standard description of the Magician as 'masculine energy' similarly drives home our cultural belief that men and masculine people naturally are more dynamic, active, outward. Whilst it's argued that these interpretations refer to 'feminine and masculine', rather than 'women and men', this language still reinforces a binary idea of gender and assigns characteristics to each side which, predictably, uphold the way we see people in society and the expectations we have of them. My approach to tarot seeks to remove the chains of these old, gendered viewpoints and position the cards as non-binary, un-gendered archetypes that may be filtered through many different gender expressions and come out in all kinds of different ways.

I discuss this a little more when introducing the Face cards, but the work of disrupting the gender-normativity in the tarot is available with each and every card.

0. The Fool

Beginning

We begin not at number 1, but at zero. A moment filled with sheer possibility; a moment in which *nothing* is about to become *something*.

As the very first card in the tarot, the Fool is about beginning a journey. As the Major Arcana unfolds we encounter 21 further archetypes, each with an important life lesson to teach, each adding another piece to the puzzle that is our existence in this big, strange, scary-beautiful world. The Fool, signifying beginnings, represents you, embarking upon a similarly epic journey. This card says *something new is about to begin*.

I've pulled the Fool card from each of three very different tarot decks, and am studying their images. The first shows a person who is about to walk off a cliff, head held high, apparently oblivious (the Rider-Waite-Smith Tarot). Next, a hitch-hiker in the midday sun, thumb out, stripy socks and pigtails, a small pack at their feet (The Collective Tarot). Last, a fledgeling bird, perched on a branch, ready to learn to fly (The Wild Unknown Tarot).

What do these images have in common? They all show a figure who is on the brink of taking a risk. A leap of faith. Each of these figures is about to step into the unknown.

Which is a perfect metaphor for the Fool – the hero (or anti-hero) that represents each of us, embarking on a journey into the tarot, and into life itself.

As card zero, the number *before* numbers, this is all about unformed potential. It is nothing, a blank canvas awaiting action, awaiting projection. As Rachel Pollack writes,[2] 'all things remain possible because no definite form has been taken'. Pollack points out that the number zero is like an egg, full of life, getting ready to hatch. But we don't yet know what's *inside* the egg.

This isn't about conscious will. It's not about knowing, or having a set and specific goal. It's about that very first step. It's bold, but it's not about setting intentions or showing steely resolve (that comes later, for example in the next card, the Magician, and the Chariot, among others). It's rather more just *not giving a damn*. Not overthinking, not allowing space for self-doubt to creep in. Being absolutely in the moment, here, now, ready to start. It's so brave.

The Fool asks us to enter into an exchange of trust with 'the Universe'. It asks you to place your trust in the unseen, allow yourself to be guided by curiosity, move beyond self-doubt and fear of failure ... and in return you will find yourself on a journey that is richer, more challenging, more rewarding; wilder, freer, less predictable, and more fun. You place your faith in the Universe and in your own self – together. You, plus the mystery of life, is a magical combination. You're set to go somewhere good.

The Fool travels light – most decks may show a small pack, or no luggage at all. You are unweighted by old stories or fears, unburdened by what may have previously held you back.

Others may look on and see 'foolishness'. Don't they realise that hitchhiking is dangerous/they are about to fall off a cliff/their wings aren't big enough to fly yet?

And it can be so scary and difficult to trust yourself when the rest of the world is saying 'no, don't be stupid, turn back, it's dangerous!' Far easier to turn

[2] Rachel Pollack, *Seventy Eight Degrees of Wisdom*, 1980.

back, not to try. Not to move forwards.

But the Fool knows something everyone else has forgotten: the world is a magical place. And it is yours, a place to explore, to name, to discover over and over.

Advice from the Fool

The Fool encourages you onwards, whilst acknowledging that this may require a leap of faith. This may come naturally to you – for example, if you feel ready for adventure, to make a change, to experiment – or it may feel scary. It can be hard, not knowing what's on the other side. What if you fall? What if there's no one there to catch you?

But that's exactly what this is about. Don't second-guess what lies ahead. Let curiosity be your compass, and a sense of experimentation and play be your map. Move forwards, despite your fears. Remember that you do not have to have all of the information in order to act. In fact, the Fool suggests the less you know, the better! This is not about having your mind made up, but being open and ready to learn, to give this a go.

The Fool is about beginnings of all kinds: big new starts in life, a new home/job/relationship, a new spiritual journey, the start of a major project or transition. A new era in your life. Maybe you're walking away from something that is done, ready to start over – or you're about to. It can also be about a smaller thing – finally getting ready to begin a project you've always wanted to do. Sending that pitch. Getting that haircut. Telling that person. Climbing that hill. If it involves some degree of 'getting over yourself', that's Fool energy.

In all cases, the Fool is your cheerleader. 'Go for it!', this card says joyfully, giving you a wave from the road. Don't overthink this. Trust your gut, trust the

Universe, and take that step.

Key words and concepts

- A blank canvas, unformed potential
- A fresh start
- Taking a risk
- Being experimental and curious
- Boldness, bravery, perhaps naivety
- Not caring what the world thinks
- Surrender
- Answering a 'call'
- Trusting in the Universe
- Overcoming self-doubt
- Embracing uncertainty
- Defying social norms and being your rad self

Some common symbols

- A cliff edge or precipice (leaving safety behind)
- Sunshine (positivity, action, embracing life)
- A dog or animal helper (because you are not alone, you are supported)
- A small bag (travelling light, taking only what you need, casting off baggage)
- Flowers (purity, innocence, beauty, lightness of spirit)

1. The Magician

The power of intention

Where the Fool showed us unformed potential, the Magician brings shape, intention, direction. In this moment, zero becomes one. *Something* now exists. This is the other half of beginning: where the Fool showed us surrender to change and newness, the Magician offers conscious will to shape it.

The Magician represents the pulling together of disparate, intangible ideas and feelings. Where the Fool says 'I don't know where I'm heading, but I'm ready to go', the Magician is getting clear, connecting to conscious intent. This is about knowing your 'why', setting intentions, consciously choosing a direction in which to head, and focusing your energy that way.

The power of setting intentions cannot be overestimated. Intention is the foundation of spellwork and ritual (the Magician is a witch and a wizard, too). Intention is the foundation of any serious project. Setting an intention means making a declaration that *you intend to make a thing happen*. In doing so, you invite in the energy of the world around you. Where the Fool said, 'I trust you. I will step forwards', the Magician says, 'Here is what I want to do. Will you help me?'

That's why the Magician card so often shows a figure holding one hand up to the sky. They are reaching high and drawing down divine power, universal energy, the sun, the moon, *magic*... and channelling it through their human body. The other hand, pointing down to the ground, earths that energy, turns it into something real.

The hand to the sky is intention. The hand to the ground is manifestation. Fire becoming earth.

> ... *everyone has access to power and energy and magic, and the variables are only how they affect us, how we choose to access them, and what we do with them.*
>
> Oliver Pickle, *She Is Sitting in the Night: Revisioning Thea's Tarot*

Very often, this card will show the emblems of the four tarot suits (Pentacles, Swords, Wands and Cups), or symbols representing the four elements (earth, air, fire and water) because this is about access to all the resources you hold within yourself. As the Minor Arcana shows us, each of the suits and their corresponding elements represents an area of your life - your physicality, your intellect, your inner fire, your feelings and intuition - and as such they represent the resources you have within yourself. Any or all of these resources may be needed to accomplish your goals. Feel confident that you have all you need.

Advice from the Magician

As the Magician, your role is to hold your vision and to bring it into being. (If that sounds like a lot... well, it is.)

Your Magician can give shape to your most treasured dreams. It is not only about *doing* something, but about doing something intentionally. Defining your vision, crafting your intention, so that it can be brought to life meaningfully.

This takes confidence. Don't be wishy-washy with what you want to do or achieve. Don't have a vague direction. Take the time to get clear about where you want to go, what you want to do; what your vision would actually look like, if it were reality.

Speak your intention. Declare it in a mural or a post-it note. Declare it to your friend. Shout it to the sky. Shout it to the sea. Shout it from the top of your apartment block. Whisper it in prayer. Create a ritual to really set your intention. You get the idea. Bring this fire that burns in you forwards, out of yourself. Express it to the world.

The Magician calls you to a position of leadership. This may mean taking leadership in your own life, taking ownership of your choices and actively shaping your story. Or, if you're working within a partnership, team or group, the Magician encourages you to step up and lead, by helping everyone get focused, energised and, crucially, in alignment with your intention.

When the Magician appears in your readings, it reminds you that you are powerful. It reminds you that you deserve to accomplish your dreams, whether big or small, and that you have the tools you need to do so. If you see obstacles in your way, find solutions, or find a different way.

It also – like the Fool – reminds you that you are not alone. Whether you are a solitary Magician or part of a team, the Universe is on your side. There is power and magic available to you. Don't be afraid to call on ritual, ceremony and other magical practices to give energy and deeper meaning to your actions.

Key words and concepts

- Setting intentions / being intentional / declaring your intent
- Clarifying your vision, centring that vision

- Directing energy consciously

- Willpower

- Being dynamic

- Putting thoughts into action

- Making something tangible

- Getting started

- Having all the tools you need

- Being powerful

- Leadership, self-ownership, taking the wheel

Some common symbols

- Four suits or four elements (access to resources)

- Magic wand (channelling 'magic' energy from the Universe)

- Pointing to the ground (making something tangible, earthing your energy)

- Lemniscate / infinity sign (transcendence)

- Flowers (growth, visible manifestation of life force)

- Yellow and red colours (passion, life, energy)

2. The High Priestess

The wisdom in shadows

In its simplest sense, the High Priestess represents the realm of the unconscious. Bearing symbols such as the moon, the sea, columns of light and shadow, this is about inner wisdom; that which we understand on an intuitive level but don't (or aren't able to) access regularly.

The High Priestess sits at the shadowy gateway between your conscious, everyday mind, and all that lies beneath. There is so much down there it can be hard to make sense of it all. Ancestral wisdom, passed down through blood or culture. Lessons learned unconsciously in childhood. Socialisation. Trauma (both our own, and that which we inherit). Forgotten wisdom, connection to nature, spirit and lunar cycles. The knowledge of body and soul. The knowledge of what lies beyond. Though we aren't always able to access this information, our bodies remember. Our souls remember. And we carry all of it within us.

Of course, it's practical and necessary to have a boundary between what sits in the unconscious, and what our conscious mind is dealing with. Without it, we'd find it very hard to get on with our day to day lives, engage with people, get things done. There's all kinds of weird (and sometimes wonderful) shit down there, and most of the time it just wouldn't be helpful to have it splurging up on the surface.

But sometimes, we *do* have to pay attention to the shadows and the mystery and the unconscious. Sometimes, that's exactly where we'll find the answers we need, or the challenges we need to face in order to move forwards. (In this sense, I think of the High Priestess as a representation of the tarot itself, and its role in guiding us towards our inner wisdom.)

How do we access this information? How do we make sense of it? That, of course, is up to each of us. When called to do so, when we know deep down that it's time to look within, it is important to go gently, with compassion and respect.

Advice from the High Priestess

The High Priestess represents a calling to 'go deep'. It can come up when you are looking outside of yourself for answers, encouraging you to go within instead.

Unafraid of the shadows, the High Priestess very often shows up to gently encourage you to look towards what is uncomfortable. So often, our fears are what stand in the way of really knowing ourselves, and it is through confronting our fears that we experience the richest kind of learning.

If you see the High Priestess in your reading, it may be calling you to confront something in your own shadow, or something you have buried deep and hidden away. For many of us, this can be uncomfortable, even painful. If we are dealing with trauma and it is unsafe to 'go there', then the High Priestess can also point towards therapy.

The High Priestess may be calling you on a spiritual journey. It can encourage you to take a break from the bustle of everyday life and to have some time out. An archetype of passivity and stillness, the High Priestess advocates a non-rational, non-dynamic approach to your situation: allowing yourself peace and quiet, meditating or daydreaming, calming the overthinking mind to allow space for a different, subtler and slower kind of knowledge to come through.

If it feels appropriate, you might honour the High Priestess as an aspect of your self – honour her guardianship of your unconscious and honour the profundity of this work, perhaps with a ritual, a prayer, or by creating an altar. It is not always easy or comfortable to do this work, but your journey will be worth it. Be careful with yourself, but don't shy away. Be kind to yourself, remembering that kindness can mean holding your own hand and shining light into darkness.

Key words and concepts

- The answer is within you

- Listening to / trusting your intuition and feelings

- Looking beneath the surface / exploring your unconscious

- Getting therapy or accessing self-help resources

- Exploring or studying spirituality

- Taking a non-rational approach

- Knowing something you can't explain

- Stillness, quiet, passivity, meditation

- A witch, shaman, psychic, or 'wise woman' figure

- Lunar cycles

- Spellwork and ritual

- Mystery

Some common symbols

- The moon (intuition)

- Water, especially still water (emotion)
- A veil (a division between worlds, or layers of consciousness)
- Scripture or text (wisdom, learning)
- A temple (a place of spiritual devotion)
- Blue and purple colours (serenity, spirituality, peace)

3. The Empress

Rhythms of reciprocity

As an archetype, the Empress is one that will be familiar to most of us. A life-giver, a creator, a source from which all life has sprung. The Empress represents the innate desire within every living thing to grow and flourish, it is every cell of our being, programmed with pure life-force. It represents the world bringing you forth, asking you to simply be.

This Empress deifies the impulse to nurture and nourish. This is fertility and growth. This is the instinct to plant a seed and give it all that it needs until it becomes a plant or a tree, producing seeds of its own. It is nature, feeding us. It is us, in reciprocity, feeding nature, tending our earth. It is cycles of life and death and rebirth. It is the care that is always available to us in nature – the wind in trees, the sun on our skin, healing rain, fruit, vegetables, grain. It is a celebration of all that surrounds us, rolling in fields of golden barley, soaking up the abundance of it all. This is unstoppable, flowing life-force.

The Empress is all about care. Self-care, and care for others. Compassion. Kindness. It is making sure your own needs are met, and meeting the needs of others. It is a dear friend showing you support. It is the careful creation of safe spaces. Creating nourishing space. Bringing people together and encouraging them to grow together.

There is radical self-acceptance here, the willingness to be in your own skin and allow others the same freedom. Empress says: 'I am here and I love myself. I belong here. I am held. There is space for me here. There is space for you, too.'

This is also sensuality, sexuality, body-love, body freedom. Skinny dipping. Strutting your stuff. Wearing what you want. Tenderly enjoying the body that you have, its unique beauties, its strengths, its limits. Working towards a healthy relationship with your physicality, playing with it, trying new things.

It is a physical engagement with the world that is anything but mundane. It is finding the magic that exists all around us; it is the pleasure of touch, taste, smell, sound and sight. It is a rose garden and a deep, hot bath. It is cake, or leather, or whatever turns you on. Ruled by Venus, the Empress is luxury and pleasure.

When you hold space for a friend, cook nourishing food, or run a hot bath for a tired lover, you express the energy of the Empress. When you prioritise self-care and look after your material needs, you express the Empress. When you tend a garden or put on your fanciest/sexiest/most comfortable outfit, expressing what is within you through your clothing or make-up, you are channelling Empress energy. When you feel the restorative power of nature, practice herbalism, talk to trees, camp out, gather flowers for your table, watch a sunset or sit in the park, you're communing with the Empress.

Advice from the Empress

The Empress wants you to love and care for yourself – unconditionally. As Empress energy is earthy, grounded stuff, this means making sure your physical needs are met. Focus on your environment, your home, your workspace – are these comfortable and pleasant places to be? Nourishing food, clean bedsheets, access to green space – these are mundane aspects of our lives, but the Empress will tell you they are foundational to happiness. It's easy to get distracted by 'higher' pursuits – spirituality, intellectualism – but your physical world matters, too. The Empress celebrates the magic in these foundations.

We all deserve to feel loved and cared for, it's not something we have to 'earn'. The Empress can represent you meeting your own needs, and it can represent giving or receiving care from others. Playing a nurturing role, caretaking, parenting, showing up for friends or strangers. The Empress represents these kinds of roles, and asks you to look at your relationship to them.

It's important to remember that the Empress has this in balance. This is not a person who only cares for others and neglects herself. Neither is this a person who is focused only on their own needs - there is a lot of generosity, a lot of reciprocity, a lot of give and take in this card. So when you see the Empress in your readings, you might want to check you're on a two-way street when it comes to giving and receiving care and support.

The Empress represents a luxurious, spacious slowness. Taking time to pay attention and tend to the details of our lives. When a seed is sown, the harvest does not arrive the very next day – a lot of love and care and time go into bringing each plant to fruition. So the Empress is about taking that time and making a commitment to supporting processes that are slow and organic. Whether that's work stuff, a relationship, a transition, a journey, the message is the same. Treat it with love and tenderness. Give it what it needs. Allow it some space and time.

This is also a card of abundance. It can show up to remind you how much beauty there is in your life, or to encourage you to get out and breathe fresh air. It's a card that celebrates the simple things – but it's also one for luxury. Allow yourself a treat or a spree, pamper yourself, let yourself feel good.

Lastly, and perhaps most obviously, the Empress is about nature. Being in touch with the world around you. Getting out there and seeing the sky. We all know that time in nature is restorative, physically, emotionally and mentally. Remind yourself that you were born from this earth and will return to it, that this is where you belong. Remember that nature loves you, and you have nothing to prove.

Key words and concepts

- Self-love and love for/from others
- Creativity and self-expression in all forms
- Abundance, richness
- Nature, cycles, feeling in tune with the seasons and the natural world
- Being in the flow
- Sexuality, sensuality, enjoying your physicality
- Fertility
- Life force
- A maternal figure in your life

Some common symbols

- Plants growing (fecundity, growth, generative culture)
- Crops (abundance, richness)
- Venus symbols (love, sexuality, pleasure)
- A crown (power, being in charge)
- Pregnancy (fertility, generation, and birth)
- A river (feelings in motion, flow)

4. The Emperor

The quality of our foundations

Many folks have a troubled relationship with the Emperor card. Plenty more strongly dislike it. According to my own (totally informal and unscientific) research, the Emperor is the least popular tarot card of all.

As the Emperor is traditionally read as the archetypal 'Father' (with the Empress as 'Mother'), there are Freudian and Jungian explanations for this that are rooted in father-child (and mother-child) relationships. As in, the Emperor can represent your own father and/or that relationship, or it could point to your relationship to masculine parental figures and paternal authority in general. (You can research the Father Complex if this interests you.)

Beyond 'Father', though, the Emperor also represents social structures, norms and codes.

Authority. Government. The establishment. The patriarchy. The Emperor can represent the rule of law, decision-making by out of touch leaders, institutional oppression, and so on. The Emperor typically prizes order, conformity, commercial success, strong hierarchical leadership. Going further, it can be about the ways law and order is enforced: this may point to the prison system, the police state, white supremacy, religion or capitalism as social control, and so on.

But the Emperor does not only signify oppressive or harmful structures. It can also be the qualities of leadership that can achieve positive change. In the Slow

Holler Tarot, this card is renamed 'Navigator', and represents a person who '...
has skills, confidence and experience that allow them to steer, direct and
create structures for group effort.' This person can talk the talk, understand
the relevant norms and codes, and is able to lead with confidence. These are
valuable skills that can inspire. They are useful in all kinds of spheres.

> *Expectations are clear, boundaries are set and marked, and all*
> *standards and protocols are laid out. Despite their emphasis on*
> *order and structure, they can also show a bold, innovative vision*
> *– their solid base of knowledge sprinkled with a dash of daring.*

The Slow Holler Tarot (co-authored)

As a leader, the Emperor can be someone who grabs power and wields it over
others, or it can be someone who is able to lead with compassion and, assisted
by a team, achieve great things. It represents the difficult decisions that need
to be made, the structures that inform those decisions, and the importance of
accountability at all levels.

Advice from the Emperor

The Emperor will often be asking you to confront difficult power dynamics as
they manifest in your own life, such as your relationship with authority,
feelings of (or very real) powerlessness, complicity in oppressive structures,
your own use or abuse of different kinds of power, and more. It can represent
any institution, person or group that wields power, or it can be yourself.

This card is also about doing groundwork. The Emperor looks at what needs to
be in place for effective work to be done, taking responsibility for the essential
work of creating solid, strong foundations upon which projects can be
successfully built. For example, the Emperor is a fantastic group facilitator,

able to craft sound containers for people to work together safely and effectively. They lead a group in establishing ground rules, then ensure they are followed, knowing that if they're not, the safety of the space is compromised and the group will not work well.

The Emperor could be a sound business policy that protects you and honours your work. Or creating a daily routine to get you through a 'stuck patch' or to beat procrastination. For the Emperor is not a person who procrastinates! They are realistic and pragmatic about what needs to be done – including the unglamorous, boring bits.

The Emperor might look like a person creating boundaries for themself. These boundaries are an essential element of self-care, holding that person's emotions out of reach of spiritual vampires or keeping them safe from a particularly toxic person or community. By the same token, it could indicate that someone's boundaries are too rigid, or are being clung to out of fear. Within the Emperor there is always the question of the role of these structures in our lives. Are our boundaries supportive and liberatory, or fearful and oppressive?

And if the Emperor does represent 'society', it necessarily therefore can represent the vision of a better one. A solid constitution. Genuine consultation. Leadership that ensures everyone gets heard and looked after.

Key words and concepts

- Rules and laws
- Structure
- Discipline
- Leadership, facilitation

- Doing what needs to be done

- Making (perhaps difficult or unpopular) decisions

- Creating solid foundations, doing groundwork

- Wielding power (for good or bad purposes)

- Oppression, dictatorship, an institution or situation that traps and controls

- A paternal figure in your life

Some common symbols

- Armour (protection)

- An older person (wisdom gained through experience)

- Red robes (strength and leadership)

- Symmetry and straight lines (structure, order)

- A ram's head (the zodiac sign of Aries, the initiator)

5. The Hierophant

The wisdom of our ancestors

We all have ancestry. We all carry within us ancient – and recent – wisdom that is passed down to us through many different ways. The Hierophant represents that special kind of wisdom. How we receive it, how we hold it. How we pass it on.

Typically showing a pope-like figure, this card, along with its bewildering name, can be confusing. The overtly Christian symbology shown in many tarot decks has meant that it is often associated with religious doctrine, study and teaching. Whilst this is indeed one possible route of interpretation, the Hierophant's meaning is far more wide-ranging than that. Its meaning will differ from person to person, as we each uncover our unique heritage and ancestry.

I'm talking about cultural and ethnic ancestry. Race ancestry. Blood ancestry. And the ancestry we each have that arises from the identities we hold. Whoever we are, whatever our identities, there are folks who came before us and who created the paths we now walk. We carry their stories, their struggles and their victories, within ourselves. We carry their spirituality, an understanding of the symbols they honoured, a recognition of the rhythms that shaped their lives. We can't always see or access that knowledge, but it's there.

In the Wild Unknown Tarot, Kim Krans depicted a raven holding a key. Stephanie Piu-Mun Law, in the Shadowscapes Tarot, shows us a wizened, bent old tree. The Collective Tarot shows a woman instructing a feminist group in gynaecological self-examination. Wisdom can be passed on in many different ways.

The Hierophant is the knowledge in you, and it is also you, as a holder of that knowledge. It is all of the potential in you for passing that knowledge on. It is you as a student, accessing this knowledge, and it is you as a teacher, imparting it. It can also represent elders and ancestors who are teaching you.

The card is concerned with spiritual initiation and usually depicts a figure who can be seen as a translator of arcane, mysterious, religious or spiritual teachings – a conduit between god and human, between the otherworld, and this one. In this sense, it is a little like the High Priestess. However, this knowledge belongs to a specific heritage, it has a particular lineage that must be acknowledged and honoured. It has been passed down along certain lines, and care must be taken with how it is then passed on to emerging generations.

Advice from the Hierophant

The Hierophant shows up to encourage you to get to know your ancestors. The folks whose blood flows in your veins, and the folks who you claim as ancestors, as witch, trans woman, Black man, two-spirit person, feminist, fat activist, or whatever identities you hold. Who came before you? Who paved the road you now walk? How might you learn about or honour these people?

An obvious interpretation of the Hierophant is that it is suggesting genealogy: researching your family tree. Think about the identities you hold and the folks who came before. A person of Irish heritage researching the Ogham is learning about the language that shaped their ancestral homeland. A woman joining a trans history group is discovering a lineage of oppression, resistance and survival that is born again in her own life.

The Hierophant celebrates all of this wisdom, but its focus is particularly on the spiritual. Researching your Apache or Celtic or Yoruba heritage means not only learning about your ancestors' lives, but discovering more about their spiritual practices, their religions and rituals, their festivals and symbols. Digging into your history as a member of the queer or trans community should involve exploring the ways your foregoers created spiritual paths, how they built and held faith, how they supported each other, celebrated and mourned. If you identify as a witch, try to find out more about the history of healers, the folklore and the magical stories they may have told. And so on.

And all of this wisdom is really worth something in the unique way you, a new person forging a new path, will translate and communicate it. This card can therefore be encouraging you to teach, or facilitate, or write. To not only learn, but to understand how these teachings and lessons play out in your own life now, and in those of others who share your heritage. As you lean into the wisdom that has been passed down to you, recognise that it is a dynamic thing. It changes as it moves through you, as you add your unique chapters to its ongoing narrative. As you receive this wisdom, consider how you will hold it, shape it, and pass it onwards with care and respect, retaining what is sacred and old, whilst being unafraid to bring your own new stories into the mix.

The Hierophant can also represent your initiation onto a spiritual path. Converting to Islam. Stepping into Paganism. Becoming ordained as a priest or celebrant. Building an altar or committing to following the Wheel of the Year. Any significant milestone in your spiritual life is the Hierophant's domain, and it reminds you that you have the support of everyone that came before you. The energy of your ancestors lives in you, but you are not constrained by their lessons. It is now up to you to forge the path ahead – *your* path.

Key words and concepts

- Ancestry

- Connecting to your past

- Honouring your ancestors

- Family history research (where family can be genetic, chosen, or other)

- Talking with elders

- Initiation into a religious or spiritual community or path

- A new start, spiritually

- Spiritual wisdom or teachings

- Religious or spiritual study

- Becoming a teacher or mentor

- Reaching a milestone in any kind of study

Some common symbols

- Key (initiation, unlocking secret wisdom)

- Pope-like figure (a conduit between worlds, a translator)

- A teacher (passing on of wisdom)

6. The Lovers

Choose love

The act of choice is the heart of this card.

Every moment in our lives is a choice-point. Every day, we make decisions that shape our lives in huge and tiny ways. Every choice we make creates change, for ourselves and for everyone around us. This is an inescapable fact — even when we do not act or speak, when we turn away, when we hide or abstain or abdicate — these are still choices, and they still have impact.

The Lovers shines a light on the energy of our choices. It asks: Are the decisions you're making in alignment with your beliefs, your values? Do you feel connected to the impact or outcome of the choices you make? What is driving your choices?

For most of us, our daily decisions land at varying points on the 'integrity spectrum'. Sometimes we make choices that feel fully aligned with our beliefs and values — these are the choices we make when we are standing in integrity, when we are in our power. Other times, our choices seem way out of alignment. At these times we know are standing in fear, shame and dishonesty.

We can feel the difference. The Lovers celebrates the sense of flow and ease that we feel when our choices feel aligned and truthful, when we are in right relationship to our lives and each other, when we are honest, when we centre our values. It acknowledges that making the 'right' choice is not always the easiest path, but it is the brave path and the one that leads to the richest rewards, the greatest fulfilment.

And so, unflinching, the Lovers asks us: What would it look like to centre your values and beliefs in every decision you make? What fears would you have to face and overcome?

Going further, the Lovers asks us to centre love and desire in our decision-making. Many cards show two people in a passionate embrace — a coming together, making love or finding pleasure in union (be that physical, spiritual, or any other kind). As the card's name suggests, this is about our relationships, and about how integrity, vulnerability, wholeness and desire show up between ourselves and others. How our choices shape our relationships. How we show up to each other, the energy we bring, the choices we make.

The Lovers can point to unconventional relationship models, 'forbidden love', queerness, or simply feeling free (or not) to love in the ways that come most naturally to us.

The Lovers is also, of course, about loving ourselves. Extending that loving unity to our whole selves — even the parts we are ashamed of. Can we love ourselves enough to respect our desires, to choose from that place?

Lastly, this card reminds us of the fractal nature of love. As adrienne maree brown teaches, 'how we are at the small scale is how we are at the large scale. The patterns of the universe repeat at scale.'[3] The Lovers makes us aware of the relationship between small and large, between the apparently small choices we make every day, and the state of our relationships, communities, societies. Centring love, standing in our integrity — such choices have the power to shape our world for the better.

---

[3] amb, *Emergent Strategy*.

Advice from the Lovers

Clearly, the Lovers is asking you to centre love right now. If you're facing a difficult decision, this card asks you to slow down and really feel into your situation, really feel how you are responding to your circumstances. Notice where you are compelled to act from fear, anger, shame. Take the time to explore different choices. Ask yourself honestly: What do I believe is right, for me?

Seek the ease and flow that comes from making aligned choices. This may mean taking a risk, telling a truth, coming out (whether in the queer sense, or in some other way). In a world that wants us to confirm, choosing to be our weird and wonderful selves always carries a degree of risk, and the Lovers bears witness to that struggle, that fear. It asks you to be brave.

Work with your values. Be lofty and bold. Think of those you admire who create change in the world by showing up in their integrity, in their power — who stand up for what they believe. What qualities are they displaying, and how could you learn from them?

Examine the quality of your relationships. If you are thinking about one relationship in particular right now, consider the way vulnerability and integrity show up in the space between you. Where might you create deeper honesty and trust? Where might you show or encourage vulnerability?

How, also, do you love yourself? Enough to come out? Enough to ask for help? Enough to show yourself compassion and stop beating yourself up? Enough to take that class you know would make you so happy?

Key words and concepts

- Love (of all kinds)

- Making heart-centred choices

- 'Doing the right thing'

- Compassion

- Partnerships and relationships

- Self-love

- Centring your values

- Unity and wholeness

Some common symbols

- Roses (love!)

- Angel (transcendence, choosing a 'higher path')

- Any two or more parts creating a whole representing a sense of completion

7. The Chariot

Take aim, and fire

When we met card 1, the Magician, we talked about will and manifestation. The union of inspiration with focused action. The Chariot continues this theme, but here we're firmly in the 'focused action' stage. If you've ever procrastinated, you'll know exactly what the opposite of this card feels like!

The Chariot represents the forward moving energy that can arise from your focus, if you actively choose it. Knowing where you want to go, and throwing your full weight behind that goal. We often see black and white animals pulling the 'chariot' on this card, representing opposing forces, working together for a common goal. Your butterfly mind may want to travel in different directions, you may have a lot of 'ifs' and 'buts', but what's important is that you get all of these opposing energies within yourself travelling in the same direction. Rein in that butterfly mind and get it under your control.

It's about achievement, victory, overcoming obstacles, especially in that outward, socially-applauded kind of way — we love stories of people who have worked hard to achieve great things. But it's also about the process, the journey that takes place way before those 'great things' materialised. For example, the Chariot represents a great artist, the card shows us not only their famous works and 'success', but also the story behind how they reached that point; the rejections, the failures, and the decision not to quit and instead push onwards, trying again. It was focus and self-belief that pulled them through, and that is the essence of the Chariot.

In the Wildwood Tarot, this card is renamed 'The Archer'. It shows a woman pulling back a bow, arrow poised, eyes fixed on her target. There is so much passionate energy in that taut bow. So much intent. It is a magical and sacred thing to take aim in this way. It's a true commitment and it requires tenacity, self-belief and plenty of energy.

Remember, though, this is all about having a purpose: that intention we find in the Magician. You can't truly focus without 'knowing your why', without being crystal clear on what your aim actually is. Whilst this is an action-focused card, the driving force behind that action, the taught bow that thrusts the arrow forward, is intention. It is connecting back to our intention, our values, our beliefs, over and over, that brings us that forward-moving energy that makes the Chariot so powerful.

Advice from the Chariot

In its simplest sense, this is a no bullshit card that gives it to you straight: Here's what it's gonna take to achieve your goal. It's going to take work, and it's going to take focus. Are you in?

There is so much you can accomplish under your own steam, if you can find the strength and clarity to focus. The Chariot wants to help you with that. It reminds you of your courage and your strength, and it encourages you to direct your energies towards that goal you hold so dear. Connect back to your intention, be clear about your *why* — this will give you the energy to move forwards.

The Chariot often points to battles or obstacles. The road to success is not always easy and you'll face difficulties and setbacks. Of course, this card urges you on. This is a card of hard work and determination, and reminds you that it's worth it.

However, the Chariot also reminds you that the work doesn't have to be *so* hard. If you are facing what looks like an upward struggle or you feel overwhelmed, again come back to your values, to your intention. The Chariot reminds us that when our intentions are fully centred and we stand in integrity and power, we create more ease in our lives, we generate the energy that moves us forwards.

Key words and concepts

- Focus
- Focused *action*
- Self-belief and confidence
- Commitment, drive and determination
- Getting super clear about your goals
- Centring your values
- Fighting for what you believe in
- Activism
- Overcoming obstacles
- Hard, passionate work
- Courage

Some common symbols

- Armour (doing battle)
- Black and white creatures pulling the chariot (focusing opposing energies)
- Riding without reins (driving forwards by sheer force of will)

- The chariot itself (movement)

- Crescent moons

8. Strength

Compassionate activism

Note: In some decks, card 8 may be Justice, with Strength as card 11 instead.

What is 'strength'? Here, we're not talking about muscle or might, this isn't about outward control or power over others. It's the kind of strength that comes from within.

In card 6, the Lovers, we talked about 'choosing love'. Strength gives us an example of what this looks like in practice. It is the power of true compassion, the kind of inner strength that we aspire to, that can be so hard to embody in challenging circumstances.

> *You turn within and see how you're doing there, and Strength works to direct or make sense of the chaos of impulses you might find inside.*

> Oliver Pickle, *She Is Sitting in the Night*

Strength shows us that kind of inner strength that is so hard to really enact. It is forgiving someone who has caused you harm. It is overcoming lust when you know that it is the right path for you to resist. It is being grateful for the learning and growth that a call-out or constructive criticism can bring you, rather than getting defensive and angry. It is choosing to say 'I love you' to the person who is throwing hate and fear in your direction. I think of Stephen Lawrence's mother, preaching forgiveness when her son had been murdered by racists. And the Delta Enduring Tarot, which depicts a trans woman putting on her headphones and, with a smile, getting on with her everyday life, whilst outside, bigots wave placards with hateful messages. It is 'We Shall Overcome', and 'Still I Rise'. It is having the self-respect and love for this whole world to refuse to be dragged down by the hate and fear around us and within.

This is not a passive person, a victim, someone simply accepting. Much like the Lovers card, Strength is the loving determination to live, to love, to be wholeheartedly ourselves and create space for others to do the same. This card celebrates emotional labour and shines a light on how powerful that often unsung, unglamorous work can be.

To my mind, it's the biggest challenge presented in the tarot. To add love to a world that so often feels filled with hate and fear. To take part in compassionate, love-led resistance. That takes real strength.

Advice from Strength

Strength asks you to go to the places of pain, anger, greed and fear in your life. It wants you to acknowledge that these things live within you, and to own them. And to pour love all over them. To 'tame them', so that your loving heart is in control. If you're struggling with addiction, Strength reminds you that you do hold the power to overcome it – but first, you have to love yourself enough to make that choice. If you're nursing a grievance, Strength gently shows you that it's time to forgive – for the sake of your own heart. If you're furious at the injustice of this world, Strength says 'Don't get stuck in your anger or guilt. Create change.' And the way to create that change, Strength says, is to put more love into the world.

If lust or passion are tugging you to make choices you know are wrong for you, Strength reminds you of what you really hold dear and encourages you not to self-sabotage. (To be clear, this card isn't anti-lust or passion per se. It's offering a way to overcome lust specifically when it will damage what you really love.) Check in with your feelings. Notice those that will burn you out. Offer them love, and override them as best you can. Remind yourself that you love and respect yourself too much to let those 'wilder' aspects decide your path.

It is so easy to let the darker aspects of ourselves lead the way, it is so easy to react to life out of fear. If you're feeling defensive about something, if you're angry, hurt, bitter, if you want to do harm to someone, if you're struggling to forgive ... work with that. Really face up to that 'beast' inside you. Name it. Own it. We all have those shadows, there's no pretending otherwise. What is the most loving thing you can do right now? How can you offer love into a place of pain?

We can choose whether or not to be ruled by these parts of ourselves. We can choose to forgive. We can forgive others for the mistakes they have made or the pain they have caused us. We can forgive ourselves for the mistakes we make and the pain we cause others.

Strength points to emotional labour and femme labour (a little like the Empress). It points to the people who are doing the caring, listening, supporting and carrying. Those who hold the labour of empathy. It celebrates their strength and tenacity and the value – often unseen – of what they do.

Key words and concepts

- Inner strength and courage
- Loving activism, fighting fear and hate with compassion
- Dignified resistance

- Emotional labour (and its value)

- Forgiveness

- Love in the face of anger or fear

- Checking in with your emotions and overriding those that will burn you out

- Accepting and loving the 'shadow self'

- Self-love

- Making positive, compassionate choices

Some common symbols

- Lemniscate / infinity sign (transcendence, magical powers, tapping into something higher)

- Lion (the 'wild beast' within us, anger, lust, etc.)

- A woman taming a lion (love and gentleness overcoming that wild beast)

- White clothing (peace, innocence)

- Flowers (love, care, beauty)

9. The Hermit

Seeking in solitude

Sometimes, the only way to find the answers we seek is to go seek them out alone. To carve out sacred space for this search, to forsake the hustle and bustle of everyday life, and to be truly alone with our thoughts.

It's intimidating, this kind of solitude. This kind of silence. It requires a huge amount of bravery and a resourceful spirit. It takes guts to be willing to face the chaos most of us carry inside us, and attempt to sort through it and make some kind of sense of it all.

As an archetype, the Hermit is someone who has done that sorting. There is a serenity and inner peace in this card, that of the philosopher or guru who has come to an understanding of life through going within, like Thoreau, or Siddhartha. The figure of the Hermit is one we recognise easily from mythologies across cultures – the cloaked figure who lives alone in the woods or on the mountaintop; the solitary witch in the ramshackle cottage at the edge of the village; the wise one our hero must go to for advice, for a kernel of wisdom that will guide her on her journey.

Like the Hierophant, the Hermit also represents teaching and/or study. Mentorship and/or being mentored. Counselling and/or receiving counsel. As the Hermit, you may be beginning or continuing your studies, or you may be assisting someone else. Or both. Or, you may be encountering another kind of guide – an animal helper, a spirit guide, a therapist, an author – some wise soul who can guide your journey.

Where the Hierophant's emphasis is on received wisdom (i.e. that passed down through generations) and discovering our position in some sort of lineage, the Hermit represents a more personal kind of quest. It is about going within. The lamp the Hermit carries is your inner light, the instinct and the desire to learn that will guide you to the answers you seek.

Advice from the Hermit

The wise woman in her cabin in the woods, the philosopher alone by the lake, these are romantic images, and they are metaphors. When you see this card, know that it is time to seek out some time alone – whether that be a full-blown retreat, or just a quiet night in. Know that you have much to learn. Make space for this to happen, claim a little time to yourself if you can. It's okay to say 'no' to social engagements. But remember also to turn off the screen, to put down the phone. The idea is to tune out the distractions and create space.

This card stresses the need to carve out space for your studies, or, if you're not in the process of 'studying', then simply to think and collect your thoughts. It is hard to be 'on the inner quest' when surrounded by constant chatter, media, to-do lists, distractions. An artist needs a studio, a sailor needs a ship … and a thinker needs a space in which their mind can wander. Do you have a space in your home that is only for you? If not, is it possible to create a little nook to call your own, a space where you can go?

Alternatively, the Hermit may be encouraging you to guide others on their own journeys. What particular lesson might you teach, and how will you communicate these lessons effectively? 'Teaching' might mean the traditional classroom kind, but could also be a writer, a YouTuber, a group work facilitator, a walk leader, or simply a friend who imparts knowledge. When the Hermit is representing you as 'teacher' it is specifically asking you to think about facilitating a learning journey, not just (for example) standing at the front of a room spouting knowledge. Think beyond what you understand as 'teaching'. Acknowledge yourself as a mentor and a guide. How will you help to 'draw out' the gifts of your students and enable them to find their way?

Lastly, the Hermit may be encouraging you to seek a mentor or guide of your own. Again, this may be in the form of a class leader, or a therapist, or a blogger, or an author... mentors come in all kinds of guises. Look for someone who has forged a path you admire, and approach them for mentorship, or study their methods so as to guide your own journey.

Key words and concepts

- Solitude, retreat
- Peace and quiet
- Giving your mind space
- Working things through on your own
- Claiming space and time for you
- Mentoring / teaching
- Finding a mentor / teacher
- Self-guided or guided study

Some common symbols

- A lamp (inner wisdom guiding you)
- A staff (leaning on knowledge and wisdom)
- Mountaintops or isolated places in nature (solitude)
- Hooded cloak (devotion to study)

10. The Wheel of Fortune

Weaving the tapestry of your life

Who or what is in charge of your life?

It's a big question, and the answer is of course a complex jumble of things. You were born with and without certain privileges which will ever influence your life events, choices, opportunities. You were socialised in certain ways. You have encountered luck, both good and bad; you have made choices, some good, some bad. Maybe you have kids, a business, multiple lovers. Your life is a rich tapestry that is forever being woven ... and you are not the only person holding a needle and thread.

The wheel of life is turning, continually. Seasons change, political parties rise and fall, generations of youngsters grow up and birth new ones. Your luck is up, then it is down. A leader is elected, then later defeated. It is sunny ... and then it is rainy. Is this stuff fate? Is there an explanation for absolutely everything? What is your relationship to change?

The Wheel of Fortune points to themes of fate and destiny. Whether you believe in free will or feel that life is mapped out for us, we all sometimes experience that sense that something is 'meant to be'. The Wheel of Fortune is an auspicious card for such moments, when things hang in the balance but you know in your gut that a certain outcome is 'destined' to happen.

Most importantly, though, it's about taking responsibility. Though there are many different ways to interpret the Wheel of Fortune – most often extensions of the rather ambiguous 'change'. The most empowering approach is to see it as opening up a conversation about creating change. Partnering and collaborating with the forces of change in our lives, so we are co-creators of our lives, rather than the victim of an ever-changing world where things happen *to* us. As we've seen, there are many forces acting upon our lives, our communities, our world. Your job is to work out which bits you can do something about and focus your energy there, taking the wheel and steering.

It's also about the interconnectedness of all things. The complex ecosystem within which we all belong. The Wheel can represent standing back and seeing this ecosystem as a narrative with many intersecting stories, a tapestry with many, many coloured threads, continually being woven. Think, for example, about stepping back and seeing a specific social issue in terms of a much wider history of oppression, or understanding a current challenge in your life in terms of all of the many influences that have created it.

Advice from the Wheel of Fortune

It is very easy, when we feel down on our luck, to focus on the stuff that's out of our hands. To complain and wring our hands and feel helpless. The Wheel card is not merciless – it bears witness to this, and it acknowledges that there are forces acting upon you that you can't do a thing about. The Wheel of Fortune advises you to look carefully at your situation and separate the things you can't change from the things you can and to focus your energy on the latter. To take responsibility for your life, to put yourself in the driving seat, and to bring about the changes you want to see.

It's pointing you to a truly magical intersection between being in the flow (change happens, let it happen) and grabbing the wheel (because ultimately, you must become an active co-creator of your own life). Notice that neither of these spaces is about resistance. Octavia E Butler teaches us that 'the only lasting truth is change. God is change.[4]' Drawing on her work, adrienne maree brown asks us 'What is your relationship to change?'[5] The Wheel raises the possibility that is possible to be both in the flow, surrendering to higher forces, *and* an active creator of our own futures.

This card is also a reminder of the temporal nature of all things, that nothing lasts forever. The Wheel is humbling when things are good, reminding us that life is an ever-turning cycle of good times and hard. And it's encouraging when things are tough, pointing out that this, too, will end.

Take its themes of interconnectivity to heart, too. Remember that you are part of a world-wide web, that you belong, that your actions have consequences, that you are part of a wider narrative that you continually shape, and that continually shapes you.[6] Consider chaos theory, and the idea that every movement we make imparts energy and influence into this world. Be aware of the great power in your hands to create change, and to receive change at the hands of others. Understand your life as part of a greater narrative within the mysteries of fate and destiny, as a small – yet significant – part of a greater whole.

Key words and concepts

- Change is happening

- A change in luck, especially good

- Predictions and prophesies

- Feeling like something is 'destined' to happen

---

[4] Octavia E Butler, *Parable of the Sower*, 1993.
[5] 'Octavia's Parables', a podcast by adrienne maree brown and Toshi Reagon exploring Octavia E Butler's *Parable of the Sower* and *Parable of the Talents*, 2020.
[6] "All that you touch you change. All that you change, changes you." Butler, *Parable of the Sower*.

- A shift in power dynamics

- Taking responsibility

- Focusing on what you can do (rather than being frustrated by what you can't change)

- All things are interconnected

- Seeing the bigger picture

Some common symbols

In traditional decks, this card bears a whole heap of mythical symbols, representing the four elements of earth, air, fire and water, and the four 'fixed' signs of the zodiac (and thus the entire zodiac). For an exploration of these, I recommend Rachel Pollack's *Seventy Eight Degrees of Wisdom*.

The most important symbol here is of course a wheel – or other rotary symbol – representing the ever-turning nature of life.

11. Justice

The law of cause and effect

Note: In some decks, card 11 may be Strength, with Justice as card 8 instead.

Following on from the Wheel, Justice draws us into a serious conversation about what is possible when we are all accountable.

This can be a cold card, in that it deals with truth,. Traditionally, it is seen as a card of 'objectivity'. In a world of fake news, hype and well-stoked 'culture wars', that may be a welcome concept — but belief in objectivity itself can be slippery and problematic. Institutional justice, the way we see it in the laws and courts that govern our societies, is not always fair, despite its claims to objectivity. 'Objectivity' is listed by Tema Okun and Kenneth Jones as a core characteristic of white supremacy culture, since it seeks to remove emotion from decision-making, and invalidates whatever it deems 'illogical'.[7] Objectivity does not make space for different circumstances, demographics, privileges, oppressions —the un-level playing field upon which we all stand. A woman who has escaped a violent relationship, who is now homeless and forced to steal in order to survive, may be locked up in prison when practical support and counselling may be a more 'just' social response. When objectivity is indicated in a reading, the Justice card may represent its exact opposite: *injustice*.

---

[7] Kenneth Jones and Tema Okun, *Dismantling Racism: A Workbook for Social Change Groups,* ChangeWork, 2001. See https://www.showingupforracialjustice.org/white-supremacy-culture-characteristics

Beyond this, though, Justice represents the balancing of scales. The payment of dues. The 'right' outcome. The serving of justice as we enjoy it in films and literature. Social change, progress. Justice is, in principle and by definition, about fairness, balance, equity.

It's about the law of cause and effect. As we see in the Lovers and in the Wheel of Fortune, every action, every choice, has a consequence. Justice is about the journey from those actions to those consequences, and the forethought that is necessary before action.

Some tarot decks, like the Collective Tarot, have renamed this card with the aim of detaching it from the oppressive, inherently unjust structures that govern our lives. Personally, I love the word 'justice' and its meaning. Justice, sword aloft, scales in hand, is a powerful archetypal figure representing a social and personal ideal. Without justice, there cannot be peace. Regardless of the injustice around us, this card asks us to get clear about our own ideas of justice, and how we can embody these principles in our lives.

Never forget that justice is what love looks like in public.

Cornel West

Advice from Justice

Ask yourself: what does justice mean to you? Without the waffle, the 'ifs' and the 'buts', what is true justice, in your situation? And how will you embody this in your life and work?

This is about thinking things through. It can be hard to remove the emotions from a situation, especially if you have been wronged or are doing wrong to another. But Justice does not ask you to do this. This is not about being purely rational or striving for objectivity, but it is about taking a logical perspective and facing up to the facts. What do you know, intellectually, factually, to be true? What do those truths mean, and where do they – or where should they – lead?

This card can point to the playing out of situations as they should, or as they were set up to. This action has that outcome; often this can be clearly seen. We know this – or we should know it – before we even begin. Think carefully about cause and effect when you see this card. Think about the consequences of your actions on yourself and others.

Our institutions of so-called justice, our courts of law, our prison systems, are built upon centuries of cultural oppression. What use is cold objectivity when people have such wildly different lives? How is it just that our laws are used to define who has a right to safety, and who does not? The Justice card asks us to look beyond the 'objectivity' presented to us by our governments, and our media, to see the gross injustice of our society.

This card asks you: what will you do to fight the injustice you see?

Justice asks you to create systems of fairness and accountability within your projects, work, community. This might be about setting ground rules, writing a manifesto, or naming people who will take responsibility for the actions of the group. It may be about doing internal work (such as personal anti-racism work), or having an accountability buddy or mentor. It might mean sharing power or passing the mic, or in turn it may represent asking for more power, or taking the mic. Be bold about steps you will take to move towards fairness, equity, equality and real justice in all areas of your life.

Key words and concepts

- Rational, logical thought, objectivity (is this helpful or harmful?)

- Binary, 'right/wrong' thinking (ditto)

- Knowing what is 'right'

- Justice, fairness, balance

- Accountability

- Social justice principles

- Intersectionality

- Cause and effect

- Cutting through bullshit

- Legal affairs (whether 'just' or not)

Some common symbols

- Scales (balance, fairness)

- Sword (rational thought, cutting through confusion)

- Symmetry (logic, structure)

- Thrones, crowns, robes (power and status)

12. The Hanged Man

The art of allowing

Like the Fool, the Hanged man is a figure few people understand. Just as they laughed at the Fool, stepping so cheerfully and so lightly towards the cliff's edge, here, they see a person hanging upside down from a tree ... and seemingly fine with that. What gives?

If you are a minority of one, the truth is still the truth – for you, at least. The Hanged Man represents independence from the flock, the willingness to see things differently, see them your way. It can point to critical thinking or awareness (especially when paired with other cards that deal with this theme) and it can represent courage.

The courage not to make snap judgements. The courage to give things time to unfold. The courage to resist the dominant culture of urgency and productivity, and to sink into slowness.

The times are urgent, let's slow down.

Bayo Akomolafe[8]

The Hanged Man can represent a sense of being 'in limbo'. Patience. Waiting. You do not have all the information yet and must wait and see what comes

---

[8] Bayo Akomolafe, *The times are urgent, let's slow down*, a keynote speech given at Global Summit in Johannesburg organised by Developing Europeans' Engagement for the Eradication of Poverty. See bayoakomolafe.net/project/the-times-are-urgent-lets-slow-down

next. Doing nothing can be so much harder than doing something. We are so used to leaping right onto a situation and dealing with it quickly – it is an act of bravery and strength to simply hold back, to get comfortable with the limbo of inaction. Slowing down makes space for new perspectives to arise, for new possibilities to emerge. Slowness allows for circumstances to be fully felt, fully understood. The dominant western culture rewards speed and thought and logic and communication, meanwhile devaluing the wisdom we find in our hearts and bodies. The practice of slowness is the art of allowing time and space for information to be processed not only through our minds, but through our bodies too. In the act of hanging upside down, the figure on this card brings their head closer to earth, seemingly grounding their intellect.

This is also about those spiritual practices that enable us to step back. Rather like an internal version of the Hermit – but whereas the Hermit physically claims space and time by going on retreat or carving out a space to be alone, as the Hanged Man, we create that space in our own minds and bodies. We create space within. Again, this is a courageous act, and it requires strength and discipline. (It can also ask us to overcome feelings of guilt or shame about taking time out.) Capitalism teaches us that we should always be 'productive' – the Hanged Man counters that teaching with its own.

Meditation. Mindfulness. Deep rest. Those adult colouring books filled with flowers and patterns. Staring out to sea. Taking a nap. Quitting coffee. Letting un-productivity be okay. Allowing ourselves to get thoroughly bored. The aim of such practices is not only to 'get some peace and quiet' but to attain a level of spiritual awareness, a genuine inner peace. The ego is quieted, the chattering mind ceases and we find a sense of peace, the ability to simply be; without judgement. Moments like these are awakenings.

It's an art form (in Thea's Tarot, Ruth West names this card 'Art'). The art of simply 'allowing'. The opposite of resistance, this card is about radical, deep, conscious acceptance of what is.

That's why the hanging person on this card often has a halo. That's why they don't mind hanging upside down. It's an active, conscious, loving choice. Doing nothing can be so much harder than doing something, slowness can be so much harder than urgency. The Hanged Man gives us a model of the courage, discipline and self-respect we need to claim space and time to allow ourselves to be.

Advice from the Hanged Man

How might you invite more slowness, more spaciousness, into your life? Where are you feeling urgent, or overwhelmed, and how might you bring a slower energy to those places? What is your relationship to a full plate or a difficult decision?

Where your question revolves around a decision, a 'Should I ... ?', the advice here is to hold back. Don't act; not yet. Don't make a decision. Remember that you do not have all of the facts. Take a passive approach, quiet your mind, reserve judgement. Simply watch and wait.

There are strong echoes of the Hermit here. How can you create peace and quiet, within yourself? Retreat, withdraw, if that feels right, but remember that this is about making space within your own mind. You might try the practices mentioned above – meditation and mindfulness, stretching, resting, sitting in nature – or look for other ways that feel good to you to achieve a sense of peace.

Seek peace from capitalist culture and its incessant demands on your spirit. Disregard productivity culture. In particular if you hold a marginalised identity, know that your rest, your self-care — particularly at times of social upheaval, oppression or grief — is a radical act. An act of resistance against capitalist culture, white supremacy, and the forces that prefer you exhausted and burned out. An act of political warfare.[9]

Let yourself be bored, unproductive. Practice allowing yourself to simply be. Know that you are enough. Know that there is nothing outside of you that can validate or 'fix' you. Accept yourself as you are, without judgement. And see what new truths emerge when you give yourself that incredible gift.

Lastly, just as the Hanged Man observes the world upside down, this card can encourage you to take a different view. How does the truth appear to you? Never mind what everybody else is thinking, what is your truth? What do you see? Adopt a curious attitude and experiment with looking at things differently.

Key words and concepts

- Passivity
- Holding back
- Patience
- Acknowledging that you do not know everything
- Allowing events to unfold
- Meditation and mindful practice
- Rest as a political act
- Inner peace
- Independent thinking, taking a different perspective
- Self-acceptance

---

[9] Audre Lorde, in *A Burst of Light,* 1988. Lorde is writing as a Black lesbian woman confronting a cancer diagnosis.

- Overcoming ego

Some common symbols

- Hanging upside down (independent perspectives, your own truth)
- Halo or other magical symbols (transcendence, enlightenment, inner peace)

13. Death

Cycles of transformation

As an archetype, Death is the great transformer. Death is the Wheel of Fortune turning. Death is the march of time. Death is inevitable.

This isn't about literal death. This kind of death is part of a cycle that we move through over and over in our lives, shedding skins, emerging anew each time, different, changed. Our lives are made up of eras, identities, chapters – each one a cycle with a start and a finish (blurry though these often are.) Death is about the finishing, the ending of a cycle ... and thus it is also about the start of something new. Death carries rebirth inherent within itself – its necessary conclusion.

Death represents a profound *letting go*, so that we can move forwards and grow into the next era of our lives. We must allow our ego, our identities, to 'die', we must accept that life changes, that we change, so as to grow into what comes next. A snake shedding its skin does not try to hold on to the old skin, pretending to still be yesterdays version of itself. It lets it all go, wearing its new skin, being its new self.

This card represents the inevitability of transformation and growth. You will not, cannot, be the person you were yesterday, last month, last year, last decade. The transition from one era, one version of self into another can be welcome, or it can be painful. You don't have a choice, it is a natural process. But you can choose whether to embrace death, to move with it, or to resist and fight it.

If we choose to move with the change Death brings, we practice adaptation. We do not resist the new reality, we accept what is, and we adapt, we change, we develop to meet the new circumstances of our lives. This process of transformation may be immediate, or it may be slow, perhaps a lifelong or even generations-long evolution. What matters is our engagement with the process. Our willingness to shed what is no longer needed, to grow into new shapes and new realities.

Advice from Death

Death appears in tarot readings for all sorts of reasons. Most simply, like the Wheel of Fortune, it is a herald of change. It's telling you that cycles are turning, something is coming to an end.

And that it's time to let go of something. Much like the Wheel, it raises questions about your relationship to change. Are you a victim, with all this happening to you? Are you resisting? Are you accepting? Are you partnering with this change, even shaping it, taking ownership of your own future?

However you are responding to change, it is happening all the time. Death asks you to pause, and to honour the shifts taking place in your life. Show this moment - yourself, in this moment - love and respect. Death marks the passage of time with ritual; honours life's changes by noticing, witnessing, moving through them consciously. If you feel that you are going through a transformation, you may choose to honour this process with a ritual of your own. You have permission to mourn what you are losing or have lost. If it feels right, show respect to what is no longer needed, the person you once were, the things that once were.

Creating an altar, journalling, or taking some time out to do a tarot reading are all simple ways you might do this. You might want to perform magic, or hold a small ritual. Maybe you'll take a week off. A party is a different and equally valid approach. Saying goodbye doesn't necessarily have to be heavy or mournful – it could also be a celebration. New year parties, birthday celebrations, transition parties, graduate balls – these are all common ritual celebrations that honour change by saying goodbye to the old and welcoming in the new.

Change can be hard. Grief is natural. Feel everything.

Death often comes up for folks who are resisting change. Perhaps you are holding on to an old relationship that has ended, or an element of your personality that is no longer true for you. It's encouraging you to let go and to look forwards. Honour this letting go, and say goodbye with love, so that you can be free to embrace what is coming next.

We must also allow other people to change (because they will anyway – it's not up to you or me). Accept that you are growing and changing every day, and accept that the people you love will also do the same. Even when it's hard we must learn to give space for our loved ones to change, to grow. It is a universal experience, an omnipresent process. If this card represents a loved one in your reading, think about how you can support them through their change – help them to honour it if appropriate, and always be ready to celebrate who they are becoming (or be ready let them go if that's what this change means).

Key words and concepts

- Personal transformation
- Starting over, moving on
- The ending of a cycle
- Letting go, shedding skin, saying goodbye

- Preparing to begin a new cycle

- Ritual to honour change

- Being in the flow of change, not resisting

- Adaptation

- Letting go of an old identity, accepting that you have changed

- Honouring the seasons of life

Some common symbols

- Skeletons (death)

- Shedding skin (change)

- The grim reaper (change is inevitable, and is coming)

- Sunrise (rebirth, a new day)

- Flowers (renewal)

14. Temperance

Magic in the in-between

Whilst the Major Arcana is filled with wild, powerful archetypes, a few cards have a a quieter, less awe-inspiring kind of power. Strength. The Hermit. The Hanged Man.

And Temperance – perhaps the least glamorous of them all.

Temperance is about going steady. The word itself means 'moderation', which often means restraint. Choosing the middle way. Not upsetting the apple cart. A lack of extremes.

By the same token, it's also about blending dualities. Often, this card shows a figure pouring water from one cup into another, one foot on land and the other in a river, achieving a blend. This can apply to anything that we tend to view on a spectrum (see the next section for some examples).

Temperance is an answer to the tarot's emphasis on duality. It is the wide, amorphous, magical area in the middle of the spectrum, where lines themselves become blurred. It's a third dimension, it's more than just one thing. This is a liminal space worth exploring in its own right, as you learn to take the disparate ingredients of your life and blend them in ways that work for you. The result is a kind of alchemy, as, together, all of these ingredients become more than the sum of their parts.

On the traditional image, the angel (who, by the way, is un-gendered, non-binary, or genderqueer) not only pours water between two cups, but they defy gravity in doing so. The water flows in a diagonal line. Powerful forces are at work here – this isn't a mundane process, but a magical one. When we transcend binaries, 'right/wrong' thinking, we enter into a truly magical space where anything seems possible.

There's real magic in this liminal, in-between space. In not being one thing, or another, but a blend of two or many things. Beyond simple 'moderation', Temperance is like honing a fine recipe. A little of this, a little of that, seeking the perfect balance, adding a little at a time, stopping to taste, to feel, to learn. Too much cayenne and your chilli won't be palatable. Too little, and it won't have any fire. It is an experimental, learning space.

We hear a lot in the 'self-development' world about achieving balance and harmony. It's something many of us seek. Extremes can be fun, but aren't always sustainable (for our minds, hearts, bodies). Temperance shows us what it can look like to really make space to learn what we need – the many different ingredients, unique to each of us – that create our 'happy blend'.

That harmony and balance so many of us seek is not a boring or mundane goal. It's lofty, and it's as important as all of those louder, more glamorous cards. It's a form of radical self-care to allow yourself this kind of space and focus. In modern life we are tugged this way and that. So many demands are made of us. So many exclamation marks, so much *awesome* and *awful* and *get this right now*. What does it look like to simply sit with ourselves, with the complex, multi-faceted beings that we are – to honour the many different parts of ourselves, to simply *see* them?

Advice from Temperance

Temperance points to moderate or halfway points on anything we may view on a linear spectrum. This might mean simply choosing the 'middle way' – even sitting on the fence – in decision-making. Or it may be about tempering extremes, however they are showing up in your life. Some everyday examples are:

- Work/life balance. Not throwing yourself entirely into work, not slacking off either - Temperance appears in our working lives as a healthy balance. (I house-sat for two weeks whilst writing the course that would eventually become this book, and I was looking forward to losing myself completely in this piece of work. I managed two days before I began to feel ill. I needed balance, to go outside, to do other things.)

- Resisting extreme choices. Maybe you want to cut a friend out of your life, or completely shut down your website, or ditch social media for good, or quit your job in a blaze of glory. Temperance advises you against such extremes. It asks you to cool your boots, and find a halfway measure or moderate way of meeting that need. Test the waters first, before going the whole hog.

- Gender. The non-binary gender identity is a perfect expression of Temperance. Not one extreme or the other (if we view gender as a linear spectrum with 'man' at one end, 'woman' at the other), but somewhere in-between. A non-binary person's gender expression may shift on a daily basis, combining elements of both genders however feels right.

- Multipotentialism. Emilie Wapnick, founder of online community Puttylike and author of *How to be Everything*, maintains that we are not bound to choosing one path in life, but can combine multiple passions, interests and skills into a multidimensional whole. You can wear many hats at once!

These are just a few examples but there are so many ways that extremes can show up in your life. When you see Temperance in your tarot readings, look for the places in your life where you could do with 'tempering' those extremes.

Challenge yourself in places where you've fallen prey to binary thinking or false dualities, and consider the possibility of multiple ways forwards, a diversity of 'right answers'.

In a simpler sense, look also for ways to invite calmness into your life, and consider your relationship to harmony and balance. How might you move towards a place of greater harmony (however that looks for you)? What do you need to bring in, let go, or 'even up' in order to feel steadier, more in balance?

Key words and concepts

- Balance, harmony
- A blending of dualities
- Alchemy
- Seeking the middle path
- Not making extreme decisions
- Taking a non-binary attitude
- Seeing multiple possibilities
- Hearing multiple voices
- Testing the waters
- Experimenting
- Self-care, grace, gentleness

Some common symbols

- Non-gendered angel (transcending the duality of gender)
- One foot in the water (testing the water, blending elements of earth and water)

- Water – being poured and in the landscape (intuition, feeling)

- Sunrise (a new day, a new start)

- Two cups (love)

- Flowers (natural renewal)

15. The Devil

What holds you down?

The Devil, often with its foreboding images of demons and chains and dark, scary hellscapes, points to the devil we all carry within us.

It asks each of us: *what holds you down?*

A common image on this card is a human or humans, chained or tied, lorded over by a demon and making no attempt to get free. They seem to accept their circumstances without question or struggle. In this, the Devil discusses complicity. It is so easy to give in to the oppressive structures that hold us down, far easier than the hard work of getting free. It's about that very human paradox in which we come to *want* the things that harm us or hold us back. Addiction – to substances, to consumerism, to 'things', to self-destructive behaviours, to social media, to whatever – is a form of putting off this hard work. We turn to external gratification when we feel a lack within ourselves, and are never satisfied. But it is easier than really dealing with what's going on inside.

In some decks, the Devil points to oppression coming from outside. I tend to reserve that interpretation for the Emperor, the Wheel of Fortune and some of the minor arcana – cards, which point to power structures that impact our lives. The Devil, for me, is very much about the prisons that we create for ourselves. It is deeply political, but in a very personal way. Whatever may be coming at us from outside, the Devil deals with how we respond.

At its most proactive, it is reminding you that you always have choices. Painful as it may be, it asks you to own your own bondage, to be self-aware. Own the stories that you tell, recognise when you are creating stories to hold yourself down, or when you are allowing others to tell your story for you, to define you. Ask yourself, 'what am I afraid of?' Because, ultimately, this scary old card is about confronting the fear inside.

Advice from the Devil

I resolutely believe that there is no judgement within the tarot (I mean, aside from the card that's actually named 'Judgement'...) But seriously. No card judges you. No card tells you 'you are bad' or 'you are good'.

What we get instead is righteously called out. As in, 'What's this behaviour about? What are you avoiding? How are you holding yourself back? And how are you complicit in structures that oppress you?' The Devil is not a gentle card, but its message doesn't have to be harsh. It is an act of self-love to take the advice of your own demon, and look it in the eye.

After that, you get to plot your escape. Your eyes are open, you are aware of your complicity in a structure that oppresses you. Now you can get free. Your ego, anxious to hold on to that easier identity, tries to replace its addiction to external validation with something else, but you can overcome this neediness. There is so much more to life.

When you see the Devil card, consider your relationship to freedom. Likely, it is more complicated than it may seem at first. We humans have a way of fearing the freedom to be ourselves, we hide from the opportunities to live into our full potential. Ask yourself if this feels true for you, and in what ways. Examine the quality of the cages you build in your own life, the ways you hold yourself back.

Consider what freedom actually means, to you. Think about the freedom you create within yourself. What makes you feel free? When are you most like your true self? How can you bring more of that energy into your life?

In that same vein, there's a more mundane message here about materialism. Addiction to 'things' is a sad issue of our time – it leads to huge amounts of waste, a throwaway culture, and a sense of not having enough (which ultimately means: not *being* enough). We buy to fill the need, to fix ourselves. Our inner demons tell us that we need 'things' to make ourselves more beautiful, successful, popular, wanted, acceptable, 'good'. The Devil can represent becoming bogged down in this stuff, forgetting about the bigger picture and what is truly important in life.

Key words and concepts

- Bondage
- Addiction
- Materialism
- Destructive behaviours
- Getting trapped in harmful cycles
- Choosing to get free — or choosing not to get free
- Losing sight of what is important in life
- Confronting fear
- Accountability to yourself
- Delusion ... and self-awareness
- Committing to your own freedom

Some common symbols

- Chains (bondage)
- Nakedness (vulnerability, poverty of spirit)
- Hellish imagery (a spiritual prison)
- A devil or demon (inner demons)
- A key (freedom)
- Upside-down pentagram (materialism)

16. The Tower

Revolution hurts

The Tower has a simple meaning: the crumbling of the status quo.

The Tower – whatever it represents in your reading – comes crashing to the ground. All that you held to be true is suddenly … not true. The world looks different, and it can feel like a disaster. This card's usual image of lightening destroying a tower is incredibly scary – destruction is all that we can see. The ground is unsteady beneath our feet. We don't know what to hold on to.

It may point to something external – like a power structure being toppled – or it might be internal, like the overcoming of a personal struggle through a momentous and destabilising change. It may be the result of a long and bloody battle finally over. Or it may be completely out of the blue.

One thing is for sure: life will never be the same again.

As Death showed us, change can be hard. In the Tower, it can be brutal. The Tower's particular brand of change normally occurs as a crisis (whereas Death's can often be slow, organic, even gentle). In the Tower, change hurts. People get hurt. You don't know what to do next. It might feel like all is ruined or lost.

The Tower can point to such an event – a seismic shift, internal or external (think of the Devil, the Wheel, etc.), but in doing so it is asking a pressing and important question: *what next?*

Built into this shattering of all that is known, this shaking of once solid seeming foundations, is the sudden new possibility of starting over. Many tarot readers talk about their own 'Tower moments', referring to those huge and very challenging moments in our lives where everything shifted. It was terrifying in the moment and the fallout might have been tough too, but later, when the dust had settled, things became better than they had been before. With the status quo blown to bits — whether we wanted that or not — we found ourselves facing clear ground to build anew.

It's time for a revolution.

Advice from the Tower

Being outed, quitting your job, getting fired, getting dumped. Getting totally called out (and being able to learn from it). These are all examples of Tower moments. Shock events that feel incredibly painful, but that ultimately move us forwards, to a point of no return.

The dust will settle. And you will be standing in the rubble, watching the air clear. There may be some mourning to be done, some goodbyes to say or loose ends to tie up. People, including you, may be scared or lost. But ... the once-mighty 'tower' that was dominating the landscape is now gone, and there is space for something new.

There is a gentler side to the Tower, too: this card can simply bear witness to your pain. You are not obliged to start 'rebuilding something better' after the loss of a loved one or a truly tragic event. Where the shock was not one that opens up exciting possibilities, but instead only leads to grief (and, eventually, healing), this card puts a hand on your shoulder and says, 'This is tough. It really is. It's okay if you feel knocked sideways.' For all it's focus on crisis, the Tower also contains the moment *after*. When the dust is settling and feelings, many many feelings, are being felt. There is space in this card — at times, almost an eerie silence — for that to happen.

Then, if appropriate, and when you are ready, the Tower is about those next steps. Preparing to rebuild. Ask yourself, what was wrong with the old way? How can we do it better this time? Dig deep and find the confidence to build a new world that is kinder, juster, more honest, or whatever it needs to be.

Key words and concepts

- Revolution
- Disaster, crisis, shock
- Mourning, grief
- Blowing apart old structures, demolition of the status quo
- Toppling systems of power (on small or large scales)
- Potential
- Making way for the new
- Finding a new way
- Rebuilding after disaster
- Blessing in disguise as disaster
- Rehabilitation, regeneration

Some common symbols

- Lightening (a sudden shock, disaster, destruction, or a bolt of truth)
- A tower (the old establishment, the old way)
- Falling people (fallout, harsh consequences)

17. The Star

Navigating the journey home

A counterpoise to the terror wrought by the Tower, the Star brings peace, hope, a light at the end of the tunnel. It's coming home. It's something to reach for, to hold on to.

In its most basic element, the Star is a soothing voice from the night sky whispering, 'everything is gonna be okay.' It's a hug that gives confidence, a cup of tea that calms and reassures.

Sequentially, this is a powerful shift of energy. We have recently met Death, the Devil and the Tower in quick succession (with Temperance bringing some relief). Things have been rough, a lot has changed and been witnessed, not all of it pretty. At this point in the Major Arcana, The Star's appearance marks a welcome change.

It brings hope and positive energy. It tells us that things are looking up. It reminds us of our own power, the great capacity we hold for healing – ourselves and the whole world. It's our collective energy of love and compassion. We are all interconnected. We contain multitudes. Our capacity for healing is immense.

The Star represents healing itself.

I always find it funny that it should be a celestial body – one that belongs in another galaxy, outside even our solar system – that should carry such comforting, grounding, intimate energy. The Star is about your inner light, the very essence of who you are – beautiful, creative, kind. Tuned-in, connected and free. So many areas of our life – education, society, career – have us creating barriers around all of these qualities, obscuring them from view. And yet, they are always there, shining within each of us. We can hold on to them.

Advice from the Star

It is a 'star', of course, because it is there to guide you. To help you navigate the waters of life. Like a sailor following the constellations, that inner light inside you will guide you home to yourself. The Star brings you the healing, steadying message that *you are still you*. Whatever has changed, whatever you have been through, that essence of you remains – strong and bright, burning within. (The Star can also represent a loved person who has passed away, reminding you that their essence and energy lives on, offering comfort and solace.)

We each contain infinite possibilities, infinite capacity for beauty, infinite wonder. When times are hard, remember who you are. Remember your capacity for healing and magic. Know that you are a creature of this earth and of this universe, that you belong here. That you are loved.

Things will be okay. You will be okay. Healing is in progress and you are doing fine. You are in then midst of a beautiful process of coming home to yourself.

Remember to be true to yourself. Be gentle. Be compassionate. Listen to your intuition, and know that your body and soul are always working to heal and to grow stronger. Give yourself the space and the care you need to do this.

If you are feeling a 'calling' right now – answer it. If there's something you'd love to do, create, try – approach it with love and give it a go. Take a positive, gentle approach to the things you do.

On a social level, this is also about community healing. Hope, compassionate leadership, co-operative working, and the ways that people in communities show up for each other, have each others' backs, create joy and beauty and magic, even in the face of challenges. Within a community setting, the Star is the glowing light of a shared identity or culture or belief, reminding folks who they are, and that they each belong.

Key words and concepts

- Hope
- Love and support
- Coming home to yourself
- Self-care
- Healing
- Being guided by your intuition
- Integrity, honesty, being true to yourself
- A positive new start or new vision
- Compassionate, cooperative leadership
- Belonging

Some common symbols

- The water bearer (Aquarius)
- Nakedness (being vulnerable, but feeling safe)
- Pouring water (soothing emotion)
- Stars (guiding lights)
- Cups (containers of emotion)

18. The Moon

All is not what it seems

When the moon shows up as a symbol on the other cards (the High Priestess, the Chariot) it is a symbol of intuition, the power of the unconscious. However, when we encounter the Moon card itself, there is a lot more going on.

The realm of the Moon is shadowy and hard to see. Secret messages, dreams, intuited information, obscure symbols and odd signs. It's that 'Is it...? Or am I imagining it?' kind of energy, that feeling of just not being sure what you're seeing or feeling.

The Moon (that great, grey rock in the sky that governs our oceans, pulls the tides and, with them, our moods) is at the heart of many, many myths. It represents mystery and madness, the unseen, shadows and sorcery.

The traditional image on this card is weird and otherworldly: two odd towers form a gateway to the distant mountains; who knows what lies there? In the foreground, a lobster emerges from the sea, representing the unconscious and the intuited rising from the deep. In the centre, two dogs howl either side of a river. One is a domestic hound, the other a wild dog; both are parts of us. Under the Moon, the wild dog gets its chance to howl.

It is scary to see what is normally tucked away inside, out in the open, using its voice. We can be afraid to allow our inner wildness – which some may see as madness – to be seen. But it is liberating, too, to give space to that untamed, unsocialised nature. To let your wolf howl.

The Moon represents witchery, spellwork, magic and occult arts of all kinds. It's rituals and ceremonies, and also smaller acts of magical intent. It asks you to forget about what is rational, what you 'know', and to delve into life's mysteries. This can be soulful, creative and profound work, or it can be simple and experimental.

The Moon can also represent lies and manipulation. We all wear masks, we all deceive and are deceived. The Moon shines its silvery light on those elements of ourselves, asking uncomfortable questions about what is true, and what isn't. What we present, and the reality.

As an archetype, the Moon also has a relationship with mental health, 'eccentricity' and neurodivergence. Whether ridiculed or revered, the Moon does not conform to society's norms. Perhaps this person hears voices, sees visions. Perhaps they are trying to tell us something and nobody will listen. Through this, the Moon may be asking us to look differently at the world. It may be celebrating neuroatypicality or divergence from society's norms. It might also signify mental health problems or challenges: whether internally or externally imposed. It might also be read as encouragement to seek support.

Advice from the Moon

There's a lot going on here, and it's hard to know what this card might be saying to you. Is it encouraging you to wake up and smell the coffee, or to give in to the mystery? Does it say you're deceiving yourself, or that you're receiving messages from the other side? Things are certainly strange, and it's okay if you feel disorientated.

All is not as it seems and, frustratingly, this is not a card for answers. It's a card for weirdness, secrets and mystery. It's up to you to check in with how that feels, to listen as deeply as you can to your intuition, and to either figure out your next steps, or give up and go with the wild, howling flow.

Don't focus on concrete answers right now, but be open to the grey areas, the swirling nature of things as truth is gradually revealed. Relax your need to know where you stand.

If you're called to any kind of magical practice, now is a good time. Get as witchy as you like, really connect to that wild moon energy.

However, if you're feeling the deception/manipulation vibe of this card, don't be afraid to dig into that. It's scary and it's hard work, but it may be time to look closely at what's really going on. What are you not seeing? What are you turning a blind eye to? What are you hiding from? Which areas of your life feel like they are lacking in integrity, or as though someone is not being honest? If you feel you're wearing a mask at times, ask yourself: is this mask a healthy boundary, or am I pretending to be something I'm not? Explore the reasons for this.

There may be echoes of the Devil here. Note that abusive and self-abusive behaviours such as gaslighting and tone policing can be indicated by this card — be gentle with yourself as you explore its meaning for you (you can refer to the earlier section in this book for ideas on self-care and staying safe when reading tarot.)

Key words and concepts

- Shadow work

- Getting in touch with your wild nature

- 'Letting your wolf howl'

- Listening deeply to your intuition

- Secret messages, signs and symbols

- Being totally non-rational

- Witchcraft, magic and spellwork

- Lies and deception

- Deceiving yourself

- Wearing a mask

Some common symbols

- Howling dog and/or wolf (your wild nature)

- Crab or lobster (messages from the unconscious rising to the surface)

- Sea, water (intuition, emotion)

- Mountains in the distance (a journey)

- The moon (intuition, hidden realms, inner wisdom)

- A mask (deception, obscuring the truth)

19. The Sun

Joy as liberation

One of the simplest cards in the whole of the tarot, the Sun, is synonymous with joy and pleasure in the purest sense.

 The Sun is a life force that beams down and blesses all it touches with warmth. It encourages growth, it brings things to life. There is so much positive energy in this card, it is beaming with it. It's the card that asks: *What brings you joy?*

The Sun is the pleasure activist's card. It reminds us to connect to life's simple joys, the things that make us feel happier, lighter, freer, more connected. It's about feeling grateful for the good things we have, realising the abundance in our lives, feeing a deep, embodied 'yes' to our lives, and saying 'thank you' on a deep level.

Spiritual gratitude is hard to cultivate at first, but in time becomes a deep and important practice. Through understanding the many forces in nature (not only the sun, but the rain, the earth, the trees and everything else) that sustain us, we see ourselves as part of a whole. We have nothing to prove, we just have to be. The Sun prods us to stand tall and accept the good fortune we have. It asks us to step up and say 'yes'. 'Yes' to life. 'Yes' to ourselves. 'Yes' to all of it.

As such, this card is about liberation. A counterpart to the Devil's themes of bondage, the Sun shows us what absolute freedom might look like. It's social message is about cultivating freedom in our own lives, choosing to feel good, to show up for life, to receive the pleasures and gifts of life, to give back in joyful reciprocity.

This card may feel like waking up from hibernation. After a long winter, we finally feel the sun's rays on our faces and awaken, refreshed and ready to move. It's the energising nature of that light, the way it encourages us to rise and embrace the day.

Advice from the Sun

This card preaches gratitude. 'Gratitude journals' are a cliche these days, but they have a profound purpose. rite a list of all of the things in your life that bring you joy, and say 'thank you' for each thing. Practice noticing the good fortune that you have, the beauty that surrounds you. Explore the possibility of positivity, and how it feels to view your life with that possibility always in mind.

Sometimes this comes naturally – the glass is half full and the future (and more importantly, the present) feels bright, it's easy to feel positive. Other times though, it can be tough to 'look on the bright side'. The practice of gratitude and the looking to what really is good in your life can be challenging. Try it anyway. There is energy there to help you.

If the Sun's essence feels very foreign to you right now, then let this card witness you and encourage you to take hold of your feelings. This isn't about 'pulling yourself together', neither is it any kind of 'cure' for depression or grief. It is more about consciously walking with the idea of happiness, knowing that it is an option, and gently moving in that direction. Knowing that you deserve to feel joy in life. Knowing that it's possible.

The Sun can tell you to stop overthinking and enjoy what is available to you. It can say get out there and grab it, or stop and smell the roses, or anything else that means 'life is good, enjoy it!' If you're procrastinating on something, you're probably overcomplicating things. Get back to the essence of the thing. What's good about this? Why do you want to do it? Let that guide you.

Consider your relationship to freedom. Where in your life could you feel freer to be yourself? How might you get out of your own way a little, loosen up a little, embrace more of the freedoms that are available to you?

In this sense, it urges you to simplify your life, your situation, your quest, your fears. Focus on what really matters, what is genuine, what is meaningful.

Above all, connect to what gives you life. Celebrate movement, music, inspiration, dance. Be curious, playful, experimental. Let yourself receive pleasure and have fun.

Key words and concepts

- Positivity
- Saying 'yes'
- Joy
- Freedom
- Practicing gratitude
- Success, things coming together
- Life's simple pleasures
- Allowing yourself to simply be
- Starting an exciting project
- Connecting to a dynamic life force

Some common symbols

- Warm, yellow rays of sunshine (life force, energy)
- Sunflowers (growth and renewal)
- A naked child or person (simplicity)

20. Judgement

Forgiveness

Now, having passed through some serious, heavy ups and downs, so many lessons, so much hard work, all those moments of clarity, depth, courage and greatness ... we reach the penultimate card in the Major Arcana. On the other side of it lies the World – the whole world – representing fulfilment, wholeness and homecoming.

But before we can achieve that lofty goal, however, we face one last challenge.

Judgement is a weighty card. Like Justice and the Wheel, it carries themes of accountability. Specifically, here, this is about being accountable to ourselves in the most thorough and honest of ways. This is about forgiveness, in the most radical sense.

Despite its threatening, Biblical name, Judgement is about love. Judgement is a call. An angel blowing a trumpet. A voice from the Universe. It is time.

It is a call to face yourself, completely. To hold up a mirror to your entire life, to see it all. To own it all. Your successes and your failures. The good times and the bad. Everything you're proud of, and all that you wish you'd done differently. It's yours – to stand in your wholeness, you must own it all, you must accept it all, and love yourself anyway. Judgement invites us into the difficult work of forgiveness.

The return on this work is freedom. Named 'Liberation' in some tarot decks, Judgement only asks you to face all that you are *so that you can transcend it.*

Self-acceptance sets us free, yet it can be so very, very hard to do, because it means facing our biggest fears – our whole, imperfect, scarred, messy, beautiful selves.

Honour all that you are. Acknowledge the present moment and all that you bring to it, all that you are carrying. We carry such a lot in this life, some of our baggage is helpful, like love and lessons. Some of it is harmful, like guilt or anger. Judgement can present an opportunity to lay down this burden – to own all that you carry, and then to lay it down with respect, with grace, with love.

You are then free to move forwards into a new era of your life, lighter, unencumbered, self-aware yet free; fully accepting your present self, its multitudes, its contradictions. There is an echo of Death here with this saying goodbye and ending of a cycle. Judgement asks you to be proactive about it – especially in terms of forgiveness. Free of guilt and anger, no longer weighed down by grudges and insecurity, you commit to living in the present, to your own growth and renewal.

Today is a new day. You move forwards from here.

Advice from Judgement

Judgement often comes up for folks who stand at a crossroads (that's the cross on the angel's flag, shown in some decks). It says: 'You have a choice. Do you want to continue as you are, or heed this call? Will you remain still, or move towards liberation? Are you ready to face yourself? Are you ready to love yourself?'

Only when we are completely honest with ourselves can we move forward.

Forgiveness. What this looks like in practice is *forgiveness*. Forgive yourself.

Own your mistakes, and let them be just that: mistakes. Acknowledge the hurt or pain you may have caused in your life, acknowledge the ways you were less than perfect. Then forgive yourself. Let it go. It's okay. You are not that person anymore, only a person who has learned and grown. Let that be.

Forgive others. If you are holding a grudge, know that it is harming you, and it is time to put that burden down. It is worth nothing to you now, it is an old energy, a dead weight. Forgiveness does not mean condoning harmful behaviour. It means freeing yourself from the repeating echoes of that harm, claiming back your power, saying 'no more'.

This work takes time. It's not often easy, it's more than simply saying, 'I forgive you'. It may take many days or weeks or months or years of work, of gradually unpicking and owning the complex fears and sadnesses that sit behind guilt and/or grudges. But, with the Judgement card on your side, you are working towards this, and you have all that you need to make it.

Key words and concepts

- Liberation, freedom, casting off shackles
- Laying down of old baggage
- Self-acceptance
- Total accountability for self
- Integrity, honesty
- Forgiveness of self
- Forgiveness of others
- Self-love
- Letting go
- Allowing yourself to move forwards

Some common symbols

- Horn (hearing a call)

- Angel (transcendence, call coming from 'above')

- People, birds or other things 'rising up' (the soul transcending, lightness)

21. The World

Completion

… And when we are finally able to do this – to heed Judgement's call and fully accept and love ourselves?

We arrive here: *The World.*

Here, we finally understand what the Fool's journey has been about.

Self-actualisation. Becoming. Becoming whole. Realising our wholeness, our completeness. Realising that we are one with the Universe, and really knowing that on a deep level, in our bones, in our minds, in our hearts, and in our souls.

The World is about completion. This may be in the huge, personally transforming way described above, or it may be in smaller ways. Completing a big project. Coming to the end of a challenging journey. It's about all the work you've put in so far, all the lessons you've learned, finally coming to a conclusion. It is a pinnacle. The final milestone. The end.

As we've seen before, the completion of a cycle carries within itself the seed of a new beginning. Death holds within itself rebirth. Judgement leads to liberation. The Tower provides us with a blank canvas. The Wheel … it turns and turns. As we arrive at the point of fulfilment inherent in the World, we are necessarily faced with the potential of starting over, completely.

We reach the World. We celebrate. Then we head back to the beginning. Once again, we become the Fool.

Advice from the World

This might be about finding your 'soul's calling', if you believe there is one. Tuning in to what you most desire. Living the life you really want to live. Becoming the person you really want to be (hint: you already are inside – in the World, you can step into it.)

Think about what the idea of 'completion' means to you. What would it look like to feel complete? To have integrated all of yourself into one, and to feel aligned with your soul's desire? This is about living truthfully – spend time considering what that means for you.

The World can also represent a goal. If you're working on something, know that the end is in sight, or that your goal is an important one and worth the hard work.

You have changed. You have grown. You have moved through a complete cycle and learned powerful lessons about who you are. This is something to honour and celebrate. Throw a party! Dance, have fun. Enjoy this incredible, wonderful moment. Be proud of yourself. You got this. You did it.

And know that all of this, all of this energy of wholeness, will soon be out of date. It will dissipate as life shifts again, taking you to a new beginning to start over. You have changed. You have grown. You are stronger, wiser and more *yourself* than when you began this journey ... and your next adventure will be different again. It will bring new challenges, new experiences. Surrender once again to this cyclical flow, be ready for change, let the Wheel turn on, remembering that you are simply the Fool, filled with infinite possibilities.

Key words and concepts

- Completion

- A sense of wholeness

- Knowing who you are in the world, having a sense of place

- Feeling deeply connected to all things

- Reaching your goal

- Bringing things to their end, wrapping up projects

- Focusing on your goal

- Celebration

- Preparing to start over

- Being ready for change

Some common symbols

- A dancer, often naked (sheer self-expression)

- Flags (movement and joy)

- Wands (magic)

- Circles (wholeness, completion, cycles)

The Minor Arcana

Whilst the Major Arcana illustrates the 'big themes' in our lives – collective experiences and universal forces, the Minor Arcana are much more down to earth.

Where the Majors showed us archetypes (for example, Death, the cyclical nature of our world, with its continuous endings and beginnings), the Minors depict real life expressions of that energy (the Six of Swords for 'moving on', for example, or the Ace of Pentacles for an exciting new start).

These cards look like life. In particular, the Minor Arcana shines light on what we *practice*. What we actually do, day to day. The Minor Arcana cards represent the 'stuff' that makes up our lives and often show human figures engaged in daily activities. Interactions with other people, thoughts, feelings, ideas, projects. The things that surround us, our work, our relationships, our environment ... everything is here. Where our cards mirror the good things in our lives, positive behaviours, successes, moments of joy, we are encouraged to celebrate. Where our cards show us our shadows, destructive patterns or habits, we are prompted to ask: What am I practicing here? What is its impact? What could I practice instead? By focusing on this micro level, these cards raise helpful questions to prompt us into deeper alignment with our values and beliefs.

The interpretations included in this section are generally much shorter than those given for the Major Arcana. As these cards mirror our lived experiences, it feels important to leave more space, more room for your own ideas. As always, help yourself to the suggestions offered here, but be fully invited to shape these cards to mirror the unique circumstances of your own life.

Exploring the Minor Arcana

The four suits

The Minor Arcana is arranged in four suits: Pentacles, Swords, Wands and Cups – though your deck may use different names for these suits. Each of the four suits represents a different sphere within our life, corresponding with one of the four elements:

- **Pentacles are the element of earth.** This is our physical world, sensuality, work, craft, our bodies, food and resources, home, environment, structures and foundations.

- **Swords are the element of air.** This is our intellectual world, the thoughts in our heads – including fear, insecurity, self-doubt – and our principles, our sense of right and wrong, of justice.

- **Wands are the element of fire.** These cards deal with the flame that burns within each of us – the desires and beliefs we hold in our core and that drives the things we do. These cards are very active, dealing with projects and battles, creativity and destruction.

- **Cups are the element of water.** These cards deal with feelings and emotion, intuition, love, relationships, loss, spirituality – everything that is the realm of the heart.

If your deck uses different names for the four suits, that's fine. The meanings will remain the same. (You may find it helpful to make a note of which suit corresponds to which, so you don't get confused, or write directly into this book.)

The Suit of Pentacles

Most tarot books and courses teach the Pentacles last. I prefer to start from the ground up. And that's the realm of the Pentacles: the grounded. The real. The tangible. The earthy.

The suit of Pentacles deals with the everyday, mundane stuff in our lives. But it also shows us the power and the magic inherent in these areas of life. So often we focus on lofty goals – self-actualisation, spirituality, emotional intelligence, intellectualism – these things are vital to a fulfilling life, of course, but beneath them sit foundations. Building blocks. It is hard to have a transcendent magical life if we cannot also witness the magic in our own hands, beneath our feet.

In the Pentacles we find themes of work, of money, of domestic life. Communities, workplaces, creative spaces. Our homes are here, our environments, nature. The things we do with our bodies and hands; making, cooking, tending, building. The suit of Pentacles is sensual and real. Here are the physical building blocks of our lives.

As we move through this suit, we'll look at how it feels to juggle projects and

have a role in our community. We'll look at issues around money and 'stuff' –
both having and not having. We see symbols of patience, of hard work, of
trading time and energy for reward or harvest. Health is here, and security –
as are their opposites. Abundance and scarcity. Charity and greed,
resourcefulness, materialism, and more.

Ace of Pentacles

Awakening to everyday magic

Aces represent opportunities and/or beginnings, and Pentacles are the suit of earth, the realm of all those things I mentioned above (and more).

So here, we're looking at a new start in any of those areas. The Ace of Pentacles can be a new job, a new home, physical transition, a new sexual relationship, coming into some money, starting a business, getting fit, starting a garden, taking up a new craft or hands-on hobby ... you see the pattern. These are all earthy areas of our lives; they're tangible, mundane, or created through physical work.

As with every Ace, the card only highlights the opportunity before you. It asks the question: 'Will you take it?' You don't have to. You don't have to say 'yes', you don't have to reach out. Still, it's probably wise to do so. On traditional decks, each Ace is represented by a hand reaching down from the sky. The Universe is offering you a gift! It won't last forever.

If you're not seeing this opportunity, look more carefully around you. It may come from a surprising corner (like finding 20 quid in the pocket of an old pair of jeans, or a stranger in the bus queue offering you a job). Aces very often arrive as prompts, encouraging you to open your eyes and see what is before you. What are you not noticing? Be curious.

A 'new start' can be momentous, or it can be small. Maybe you want to move house to a whole new area ... or perhaps you just want to redecorate your bedroom. Maybe you want to totally transform your body ... or perhaps you'd rather focus on having a happier relationship with the one you have. Maybe you're gonna take on some land and grow vegetables for the whole community ... or, instead, start growing herbs on your apartment windowsill. Maybe you're gonna quit your job and start a new business ... or, on the other hand, perhaps this is about asking your boss to promote you or offer you new responsibilities.

Which of the 'earthy' areas of your life – like work, money, home, body, sex, environment, craft, nature – is calling to you right now? Where do you feel called to put your focus, your energy? The Ace of Pentacles says go for it. Start where you are. Use what you have. It is enough.

Say 'yes'! Begin. There is life force in these decisions, no matter how big or small they feel.

As an earthy Pentacles card, this Ace also reminds you of the journey from beginning to end. Starting something does not guarantee your end result, your harvest. Think of it like planting a seed. You don't just put it in a pot and run off to celebrate – you've got to show up each day, make sure that plant is getting water and light. When it gets bigger, you might need to give it support, or move it to a bigger pot. It takes care and hard work, it takes real nurturing, to bring your seeds to fruition.

Don't expect instant results when you see this Ace – it's often not a very glamorous card, but more one of steady commitment. Appreciate that there is magic in this kind of work, and be ready to step up and commit. Always remember: actions speak louder than words. Having plans is great, but putting them into action, manifesting them — this is where the magic happens.

Two of Pentacles

Finding your balance

This card often shows a juggler – someone who is holding more than one 'ball' at once. Here, the juggler's balls, or Pentacles, represent projects, roles, responsibilities. There's magic in being able to spread your focus, in not dropping one ball while you concentrate on another.

It's not usually a stressful situation, though. There's a buzz that can come from keeping all your plates spinning, and this isn't necessarily about having 'too much on'. It's more about finding that balance between the different roles you hold. Getting a good work/life balance, for example. Seeing both of your partners enough. Being a great parent, but getting enough me-time, too. That kind of thing.

Twos mean dualities. How we handle decision-making, how we unify or celebrate opposites, how we work with the power of more-than-one. Here, that looks a lot like being busy! But, handled well, this can also mean enjoying the buzz of wearing a few different hats.

In a reading ...

You've got this – don't worry. The Two of Pentacles reminds you that you're capable of tricky things (heck, you're capable of really hard things). Don't shy away the moment you're pulled in two (or more) directions – this could be a really fulfilling situation for you.

Wherever possible, seek balance. Look for that sweet spot where you know you can juggle your responsibilities. This might mean getting some practical support: a desk to work at, someone else to cook dinner, some kind of time management system. Get the foundations in place so you can juggle with ease.

And if things do feel like too much? This card says 'put something down'. Juggle merrily, but don't stress yourself out. Figure out your capacity, and stay within it.

There is another interpretation of this card, however: choice. All of the tarot's Twos deal with choice. If you see this card in the midst of a tricky dilemma, it's make your mind up time! Before you do this, though, have a serious think. Is it possible to have both?

Three of Pentacles

Teamwork

Like shining cogs in a fantastical machine, each of us has a role to play in this world. From volunteering in your community to your specific job at work, making the cake for your friend's party to starting a blog, you have something special that only you can bring to this world.

The Three of Pentacles highlights your unique skills as they relate to a wider group. Maybe you're already part of that group, or maybe not. This card asks you about your skills and your role, how you can bring those skills together with other people, in order to create something great or cool.

It's a celebration of community effort, teamwork. Some of us are natural team players, others are more like solo artists. This card is one for the team, and it reminds us of the magic that can be achieved when we work together towards shared goals.

In a reading ...

This is about all things community or team -related. It's pointing to groups, families, project teams, gangs of friends. When you see this card in a reading, look at the surrounding cards. Where does the 'group' come through in your situation?

Further, the Three of Pentacles often highlights the way that everyone is different, yet together, becoming more than the sum of their parts. A healthy team or group has built in support – each member giving and receiving support from the others.

Have a think about your preferred working style. If you're a team player, great! But if you're more of a lone wolf, that's okay, too – there are still ways you can work as part of a group or contribute to something bigger than yourself. Think about the boundaries you need in place in order to do this. Embrace the possibility of being part of something bigger.

This card can bring all kinds of teamwork advice. Delegation is a big one. Remember that you don't have to be brilliant at everything, and even if you are brilliant at everything, you don't have to do it all yourself! It's easy to be precious or defensive about our work, but the Three of Pentacles shows us the magic of teamwork. Allow others to take some of the weight.

Appreciate that all of us bring something different to the table. You may be amazing at graphic design but suck at copy writing. So – find someone who can write to work with on that flyer. Maybe a member of your group is just hopeless at the task they've been set? Help them find something different to do, and assign that task to someone who can do it. This advice goes for yourself, too! Play to your own strengths and/or encourage others to play to theirs. Facilitate an environment where others feel safe to share their gifts.

Lastly, this doesn't have to be about actual teamwork the way I've described it so far. You can imagine that the whole world is your 'team'. Another important focus for this card is that of defining your own role. What do you bring to this world? What unique skills do you possess? How can you use and share them with the world.

Four of Pentacles

Protecting what is yours

This card can go one of two ways: it's either about greed, or it's about self-care. Either way, it's highlighting focus on self.

As a culture, we have a funny relationship with the concept of 'selfishness'. We're all, to a fair degree, selfish beings – we work towards our own goals, we spend our earnings on things that make our own lives better, we view life from our own perspectives. At the same time, to be called 'selfish' is a terrible insult. The Four of Pentacles raises questions about that.

It can represent a person who is being mean and grabby. Focusing on their own material gain or comfort, perhaps to the expense of others. Overly concerned with material or financial things. Losing track of what's important in life, becoming disconnected from life's pleasures. In Pamela Colman Smith's version of this card, a figure sits hunched over a large Pentacle. Pentacles cover their feet (separating them from the earth). They sit with their back to the town, forsaking their community. They look hungry and defensive. It's a pretty bleak image of greed!

On the other hand, perhaps this person is acting wisely. Maybe they're all spent out and need to save some cash to make sure they have next month's rent. Maybe they've spent so much time caring for others, they've forgotten how to take care of themselves. Maybe they're creating boundaries to help them do that. Context is everything with this card.

In a reading...

You may be getting called out for being selfish or greedy. Being too materialistic. Focusing on your own needs too much, and neglecting others. This is a frequent interpretation of the Four of Pentacles. If it shows up like this in your reading, you know it's time to lighten up. Share a little. Practice gratitude and let it lead you to generosity. You needn't hold so tight to what you have. It's not all about you.

Think also about what you might be feeling protective over, and why. When we guard our 'stuff' this closely, it's usually because we're afraid it may be taken away. Is this an idea you could dig into? Can you see what's at the heart of that fear? Explore how themes of abundance and scarcity show up in your life.

This card may also/alternatively be about boundaries (... which, of course, others may perceive as 'selfish'). There's a huge amount to be gained from accepting that you have needs (especially but not exclusively material needs), and from actually prioritising them. Sometimes you have the resources and energy to help everyone around you, or to say yes to social events, or to invite folks into your space. Other times, it's important to create boundaries, so that you can sustain yourself. This is an especially important concept for activists and folks with caring responsibilities – your work involves caring for others, but you won't be able to do that if you haven't first taken care of your own needs. When you see this card, don't be afraid to rein it in and focus on yourself.

Five of Pentacles

Survival mode

This is one of the Minor Arcana's toughest cards. The image often shows a person or people who are in an apparent state of crisis. Clothes in rags, out in the cold, overwhelmed or tired out; this is not a happy sight.

It's a card for those times when we exist on only the basics, just making it through. We may be suffering ill health, or it may be financial poverty. We may be burned out or let down. We may be depressed – with or without clear reason – or feeling under pressure. Whatever's going on, it's getting us down.

In particular, this card can point to a feeling of being left out, or even cast out. Of a group to which you once belonged. Of society, which does not value folks such as you. Of a system that was created for the benefit of just a few. There is an 'otherness' in this card, an 'outsider-ness'.

If you can understand the concept of privilege – in the many different forms it may take – then you can understand this card. This is showing us the opposite of privilege.

Some decks not only show 'suffering people' on this card, but also a possible 'salvation'. In traditional decks, for example, two figures in rags pass by a brightly-lit church window. Why do they not step inside and warm up? Surely they will be offered blankets and soup? The thing is, we don't know. Perhaps they have just that moment been cast out of that very church. Perhaps they are so caught up in their pain and struggle that they don't see the opportunity.

Perhaps they can't turn to that particular source of support because they don't feel safe in a church environment. Perhaps they are choosing martyrdom.

We don't know, is the thing. In this way, the Five of Pentacles sometimes raises more questions than it offers answers.

In a reading ...

The meaning of this card may be very obvious to you: if you're ill or getting over an illness, if you're experiencing depression, if you're going through a rough patch, the Five of Pentacles is a witness to that. It need not be anything more.

But, of course, there may be more.

Maybe you're in 'survival mode'. You have an overwhelming sense of lack, of poverty in some or many areas of your life. Every day you're just getting through it. This could be for any number of reasons, but as is so often the case in the tarot, the Five of Pentacles asks you to consider what you might do to change your situation. Depending on circumstances, this may be as simple as adopting a more positive attitude, or it may be as challenging as asking for help.

Take an honest look at your relationship to any pain you are suffering right now. Harsh as it may sound, this card often points to a 'victim' mentality, in which we take on pain and suffering as part of our identities. We choose not to accept help or solutions, because we have become attached to that struggle. On some level, we may not actually want to solve (or try to solve) our problems.

The Five of Pentacles may be pointing to ways in which you are disadvantaged. An obvious example would be a society or system that privileges some people and not others. Those with privilege enjoy comfort and security. Those who are disadvantaged suffer a lack of these essential things. If this feels appropriate in your reading, let this card open up a conversation about the role of privilege and oppression in your life.

Six of Pentacles

Dynamics of give and take

Following on from the Five, the Six of Pentacles shows us the flip side of that suffering and disadvantage. Here (in the Rider-Waite-Smith and other traditional decks) the two people dressed in rags are kneeling on the ground whilst a rich-looking person drops pennies into their outstretched hands.

The Six of Pentacles deals with power dynamics as they manifest in everyday life. The dynamics within charity. The politics of give and take, need and plenty. This is about socialism and the welfare state. It's about redistributing wealth. It's about sharing what we have – giving when we have more than we need, and asking for help when we don't have enough. It can point to healthy expressions of this kind of give and take, and it can point to dysfunctions, too — the image of a rich man dropping coins into outstretched hands does not represent a healthy, just economy. 'Charity' is not always a healthy situation (think of the expectation that people with immigrant backgrounds be 'grateful' or 'good'). What is expected in return for that charity? And who is really benefitting – the folks who need support, or the 'giver'? Who virtue-signals their generosity?

Questions may also be raised about the recipients. It may be that they have become so used to receiving handouts that they have forgotten their own power. The time of needing support may be long gone, yet they do not notice that their strength has returned, and don't stand up and take hold of their own destiny.

And then, in many decks, we see a set of scales. This is a tongue-in-cheek reference to the many imbalances this card might contain, asking us to look closely at the power dynamics of which we are part.

In a reading ...

This card firstly asks you where you stand in relation to this scene. Are you the 'needy person', hands outstretched for charity? Are you the wealthier person, measuring out your gift? Are you a bystander, watching the scene but not directly involved? What is your complicity in the complex politics of give and take?

It can of course point to the healthy kind of giving. Maybe you have spare money or resources, and you donate what you don't need. This can be a fine thing – the Six of Pentacles encourages you to spread your good fortune around.

The same goes for asking for help when you need it. We do not all have equal resources and privilege at the same time. If you need help, reach out. Don't be ashamed to ask a friend for a bed for the night, or your community to help fund your project.

But, remember the scales. Be conscious of power dynamics. Be thinking about who holds power and privilege, what is expected in return for gifts given — the perhaps unwritten rules of this exchange.

The Six of Pentacles also talks about power dynamics in our intimate relationships. It asks you to consider the role of balance within your relationships. Are you the person who is always giving? Or the one who takes and takes? Perhaps you are in a codependent relationship that is becoming harmful. Take a brave look at the balances and imbalances within your relationships. How can you and your loved one/s address power imbalances, and bring things to a more balanced and healthy place?

Perhaps you require additional support and care from friends, family or partners – or a loved one requires support and care from you. In this case, the Six of Pentacles points to those dynamics, and any underlying frustrations or resentments that can of course be present within those relationships.

As always, nobody is being judged – this is about taking a good look at what is going on, and ensuring our relationships are as healthy as they can be.

Seven of Pentacles

Pause and reflect

Remember the Ace of Pentacles, and its message of allowing time, space and nourishment for your projects to come to fruition? The acknowledgement that the planting of seeds requires commitment to the long haul, the journey?

The Seven of Pentacles shows us a midpoint. You have put in work, things are growing well, and it looks as though there will be a good harvest. Well done! This is a moment to be proud of. There is more work to be done before the fruit is ripe, but it is an achievement to have got this far.

It's also an opportunity to press pause for a moment. To step back from your work and have a think about what comes next. This might be a turning point, or it might not. It might be time to change direction, alter your approach or just make some small tweaks. Or, you may find that things are going great and you don't need to change a thing.

In a reading ...

Whatever you're busy with right now – take a moment. Step back. With your nose pressed up against your Very Important Work, it can be hard to see what's needed. The Seven of Pentacles asks you to take your time. Get the bigger picture, a wider perspective.

Celebrate your achievements so far! Things seem to be going well. This may seem obvious, or you may not be feeling that sense of accomplishment right now – either is fine. Know that you are doing great, that you've got this.

But take this as an opportunity for a turning point, too; a chance to make changes and tweaks.

Take a moment to refocus on your goals. Where are you trying to get to? Do you still want to go there, or have things shifted a little (or a lot)? Have circumstances changed since you set out? Have you changed? (Hint: you have.) It's okay to turn a corner. Remember that you don't have to follow the path you defined at the start of all this – every journey involves learning, and that may mean changing tack. Allow yourself the space to consider this.

If things aren't feeling great – don't give up, not just yet. Think about how you might do things differently from now on, how you might fix what isn't working. Look for practical solutions to the obstacles you're facing. Step back and take that wider view, get things in perspective.

This card has a slow, gentle, organic kind of energy. Take your time here, there's no rush. Rest if you need to.

Eight of Pentacles

Process

Sticking with this theme of work – especially hard and fulfilling work – the Eight of Pentacles shows us what can be accomplished if we really set our minds to something.

Contrary to the myth of the 'naturally gifted', nobody is born with the ability to create perfect works. Musicians must learn to play their instruments, practice, mess up, try again, before a perfect symphony is offered to the world. A sports star trains every day for that medal. I studied and wrote about tarot cards for many years before I felt ready to write this book (and still now, I know it's not as perfect as I would like! I like to think in the future, I will write it all again, even better than now).

You catch my drift. Honing your skills is a process – this card witnesses and celebrates that process and all the work that is involved.

In a reading ...

Some goals come easy, but most require diligent work. As with so many of the Pentacles cards – but here more than in any other – we are encouraged to take our time, and practice.

Be realistic about the work that you will have to put in to achieve your goals. You might need discipline. You might need to create routines or structures to help you make space for this work. You might need to study more.

Don't be afraid of failure. If your first shot doesn't turn out the way you want it to – try again! Keep going. Remember that practice makes perfect and, with every step, every attempt, you are getting better at what you do. And y'know, maybe 'perfect' doesn't exist at all. You might not get immediate results, but you are honing a craft, and this is a process.

When you see the Eight of Pentacles, be ready to lose yourself in process. Drop your focus from the goal way out ahead to the thing in your hands, the present moment. Be where you are, doing what you are doing, and honour the process, the journey of this work. Relax ideas of perfectionism so that you can lean into the learning and the experimenting that happens at this stage. You do not have to create a perfect finished thing today — instead, your work is to show up, be humble, and keep trying.

On the flip side, this card carries a gentle warning about isolation. Remember that there are other things in your life – good things! Whist this card isn't explicitly about taking a break, it reminds you to take care of yourself and bring more balance into your work, making sure you get rest, social engagement, nourishment, good food, and so on. Don't cut yourself off entirely.

Nine of Pentacles

You can have good things

This is a card of success and accomplishment. It represents the achievement of that kind of confidence and security that comes from having created something solid, something real, that you can now relax and enjoy.

I sometimes think of this as the 'independent woman' card, in that it is imbued with all that proud, resilient, strong energy in the archetype of the independent woman. Someone who has defied society's expectations and limitations and broken the mould, achieving strength and security on their own terms.

Like many of the Pentacles cards, the Nine points to work. We need a lot of self-belief and dedication to craft lives and projects we can be proud of. This is an end point to celebrate and enjoy, but it carries within itself the journey that led to this point. It's a proud moment where we can look back on the story so far, from this position of having really achieved something.

It's a card of abundance and gratitude. It represents feeling rich and strong in a really good way, having earned good things and appreciating them.

In a reading ...

Know that you have skills and resources that are all your own. They belong to you, and are available for you to use. Don't be afraid to use your skills.

Know also that you can be proud of what you've achieved. Take a moment to celebrate the life you have created for yourself. Ground yourself in the good things in your life, know that they are nourishing your roots.

You are allowed to have good things, and to enjoy them. You have permission to feel abundant, to feel proud, to feel rich.

If this card represents a goal for you (rather than a present reality) take this card as encouragement. You have what it takes. You can build the life you want. Take stock of your skills and resources, and think about how you can use these.

Create your own rules in life. Write your manifesto, and work out how you can structure your life in a way that works for you, that supports you to do the things you want to do. Make sure you're creating sturdy foundations upon which to build the life you want. Employ plenty of practical common sense.

The Nine of Pentacles can also be specifically about going it alone. Where the Three celebrated teamwork, this is more about what you can achieve by yourself. Trust your own voice, and don't be afraid to break away from the herd or the group if there is something special you want to go for.

Ten of Pentacles

Magic in the foundations

In the Ten of Pentacles, we seem to have it all. Life is abundant, comfortable. There is enough to go around, we are all well fed, we all have roofs over our heads and satisfying, enjoyable work.

In this suit, we have seen the planting of seeds. We've seen what it takes to nurture and grow those seeds and work towards goals, harvesting the fruit of our labours. We've talked about material resources, teamwork, give and take. We've practiced and worked hard and reached this point of really achieving something. Things have manifested. Things are good.

Now, we receive a reminder of that central idea in the Pentacles suit: the magic. The magic in our everyday lives, in our work, our communities, our relationships. The magic that we exude through simply living our lives, and the magic we receive from our environment.

As the culmination of the Pentacles suit, the Ten asks: when you have it all – what next? What else is there?

The Pentacles suit leads us on to the other suits – Swords, Wands and Cups. We'll focus on thinking and feeling and becoming ourselves on more spiritual levels. Here, we see the culmination of a long journey of foundation-setting. Now, we are ready to go further, and deeper. The Ten is the completion of one chapter, but it is also setting the stage for the next.

In a reading ...

Celebrate what you have. Feel abundant, feel rich. Enjoy the good things in your life. You deserve all that you have and it's good to just relax into that kind of security, to know that you are held.

At the same time, don't lose track of the real magic in your life. Don't get caught up in material acquisition (important though it is to have comfortable foundations), so that you lose sight of the more spiritual elements of your life. Be proud of the material abundance you enjoy – but see this as a foundation upon which to stand and look to greater things.

Tens are endings. The final card in each suit's numerical sequence, each Ten shows us a cycle coming to a close. There has been a journey, you have a story to tell. Work has been done. Lessons have been learned. It's a point where you can look back and appreciate that story, before looking forward to what comes next. The energy is about to shift.

The Ten of Pentacles represents a journey that so far has been earthy, grounded, and tangible. What comes next will feel different. Know that you've got solid foundations to stand on as you prepare for the next ride.

The Suit of Swords

Reaching the suit of Swords, we enter the realm of intellect, and the element of air. In this suit we find everything that happens in the mind: vision, planning and strategy, communication. The essence of Swords is like standing on top of a mountain on a crisp, clear day. You can see for miles, and it's a great perspective. You can see where you're going and where you've been. You communicate exactly what you want to say, and you are understood.

Here, we find justice in its purest, most unequivocal form – think of how we often see a sword in the Justice card itself. Swords are sharp and cut through bullshit, pare away fluffy grey areas and get right to the heart of what is happening. This is real clarity, razor-sharp truth.

But as we all know, the human mind is often its own worst enemy, and so within the Swords we also find fear, insecurity, self-doubt, self-deception. The tricks that our minds play on us. The battles we do, body and soul against mind. Some of the tarot's toughest cards appear in the suit of Swords.

And there is sorrow here, too – in the Secret Tarot this is named 'the suit of sorrow'. Here, we find where the mind and the heart collide, and see heartbreak and sadness. We see moments of despair, but we also find the strength that can be gained from processing life's tough lessons and growing wiser.

Ace of Swords

New perspectives

This card is the very essence of the element of air. A single sword, held aloft, like the other Aces - this is bringing you an opportunity. Wielded well, this big, sharp sword is a tool for cutting through confusion and getting to the core of things — it is a tool for liberating the truth.

A new perspective is coming through. Perhaps you're seeing things from a different angle, having big realisations, or feeling finally able to put into words that *thing* you've been wrestling for so long. It's a moment of clarity, where you can finally see things as they are.

The Ace of Swords can represent a new truth. Perhaps this is the moment when you finally find the strength to define, even speak, your truth. Maybe this truth is painful – to yourself, or to others. Recognise that pain, work with it.

Writing, journalling and letters are all implicit in the Ace of Swords, and this may be bringing you encouragement to think about how you'll tell your story. Don't be afraid to use your voice, your words. Communication is an important theme in this card. How can you best communicate what you know?

Study, learning, and teaching are important themes too. The Ace of Swords may herald the beginning of a new stage for you in any of these areas. Is there an area of your life where you crave knowledge? Is there something you'd like to study? Or are you called to teach what you know?

The Ace brings clarity, encouraging you to take a rational approach to your situation. Focus on what you know to be true, and think things through from there. Consider what is fair and just, what feels right to you — take care to stand in your integrity as you lift that powerful sword. It may help to look at your situation from new angles, seek out new information. Engage your critical mind here — not to become lost in critique, but to get clear about what you believe, what you know, so that you can act from a position of truth.

Two of Swords

Mental boundaries

The Two of Swords gives us a picture of what it can look like to turn inwards, to our own thoughts, and then beyond them. It's about shutting out distractions and really quieting all the voices outside and inside our own minds.

It's rare to experience a truly quiet mind. We are constantly receiving messages, constantly communicating on many levels. It's easy to take on others' viewpoints and forget to feel our way through to our own. The Two of Swords is about claiming that space – sometimes to the degree of cutting ourselves off completely – so that we can listen to our own truths. (This can, by the same token, be about focusing too far within, and losing track of the wider situation.)

We often see a moon on this card. A symbol of intuition, this reminds us that this is not a purely mental process. The need to turn within can come from a deep place; we may be called to do this work, to make this space in our minds for unconscious wisdom to rise up.

In a reading ...

What mental boundaries do you need in order to do this work? What needs to be quieted, or shut out completely? What voices do you not need to hear right now? It's okay to say 'no' to these voices, to silence them in your own mind. Unfollow, unfriend, mute, block – this applies to online life as much as anything. Turn off your phone or computer, take an internet break. Stop obsessively scrolling or following the news, just for a moment. Give yourself that peace.

It also may be helpful to take up or return to a meditation practice, claiming regular time to deep dive into your own unconscious, and practice quieting all those 'busy thoughts'.

Be careful of becoming totally isolated in your thoughts – this card may be encouraging you to get out of your own head for a bit, to open your eyes and look about. Your perspective may be one of many, and it's important not to lose sight of that – the Two of Swords can point to a situation where you're refusing to hear something that you really need to hear, that you're shutting out an important truth. It may be uncomfortable to hear this – but it's time.

If this card makes you feel uneasy, it may be time to put down the swords and open up a little.

Three of Swords

Scarred, yet strong

The Three of Swords is a bleak-seeming card, and its message is a tough one. It signals heartbreak, sadness, loss and grief. Often, the image is a very simple one – a heart, shot through with swords. Because this is how it feels to be heartbroken – as though your very core has been pierced.

And yet — this is also a card of resilience. The heart does not truly break, but mends itself. We carry on our hearts the scars of all kinds of battles, all kinds of pain. And we are still here. Our hearts are still beating.

In a reading ...

The Three of Swords witnesses your pain. If you are heartbroken or are going through any kind of loss, this card does not beat about the bush or pretend things are – or are going to be – okay. Shit is painful right now, and you are really feeling it. *Please feel.*

But it is also a reminder of your strength and resilience. The Three of Swords doesn't preach '*be* strong' – instead it allows you to collapse and feel your pain. You don't have to do a thing except feel. This card simply reminds you that you *are* strong. That this, too, will pass. And your heart will keep beating and you will keep growing and there is life on the other side of this.

You may even be wiser for your experience. Perhaps one day you will wear your scars with pride. This card can point to a heart that has many scars, but that is going strong.

If you are in pain right now, know that there is no rush. Healing is non-linear and may take a long time. Let the process happen naturally, feel what you are feeling, and allow your heart to do its thing. Know that it wants to heal, and that it will.

Four of Swords

Give yourself a break

Like the Two, the Four of Swords is about quieting your mind. Here, though, it is purely about rest.

Like our bodies, our minds need rest in order to recuperate strength. You don't reach your answers by only *thinking thinking thinking,* but by thinking, resting, feeling, processing, then maybe thinking some more. It is in periods of rest that some of the best ideas are born, when the mind is left to its own imaginative devices and has the space to process in its own way. (In this sense, the Four of Swords can point to creativity and lateral thinking.)

This card is imbued with a spiritual tranquility and stillness. Sometimes showing a person resting inside a church interior, it points to the kind of rest we can get when our souls are at peace. We tune out from the bustle and into a more spiritual, inner peace. The Four of Swords can lead us to a deeper spiritual practice, allowing us to overcome a chattering, worrying ego and feel peaceful and connected.

In a reading ...

This card often appears when a person is mentally exhausted. It says, 'Hey, you're tired! Take a break.'

Chill out. Really, give your mind a rest. If you're deep in studies, if you've been engaged in some kind of battle, give yourself a break and allow your mind some time to recuperate. The Four of Swords can be a holiday or a change of scene. It can be sleep. It can be retreat. It can be a Netflix binge. It can be going camping.

Practice basic self-care, especially if you feel stressed right now. The simple things: breathe. Stretch. Take a nap. Drink water. Stop for a moment and have a quiet cup of tea. The world will not stop turning if you allow your mind a break.

Like the Two, the Four of Swords applies its lesson to online life. Again, unfollow, unfriend, mute or block. Turn off your phone, your emails. Take a social media hiatus. Consider your current relationship to the internet – sometimes you can just get too much information and that may be the case here. Slow things down by getting rid of the incessant need to click and scroll, close your eyes, or lift them to the horizon outside.

If there are spiritual practices that you find calming, do these. Allow your mind to be still as you do something magical, or creative, or devotional – something that comes from a place other than the mind. If you enjoy exercise, then physical activity – the kind that requires no thought – is recommended now. Even if you're not into exercise, getting into nature is still a good idea, getting you out of your head and opening up other kinds of awareness.

Five of Swords

Choose your battles

Sometimes, we get so lost in the details of the battle, we lose track of what we're actually fighting for. The ins and outs, the he-said-she-said, the petty (or not-so-petty) grievances become the thing itself, rather than difficult moments in a wider story.

The Five of Swords shows us this scenario. It's about a battle in which there are no winners – typically, even if someone seems triumphant, by then it was over anyway. There may 'officially' be a winner and a loser ... but from over here it kinda looks like everyone lost.

When we feel insecure or defensive, it's easy to get hung up on the wrong things, fight the wrong people, play it small and petty when there's something bigger going on. This can be a defence mechanism protecting us from accepting what's really going on, or it can be a distraction put in place by a power that wants to keep you small. Divide and conquer is a time-honoured battle tactic, in which leaders and warmongers set communities against each other to distract from their own power-hungry actions. This dynamic may be as huge as a civil war, but it also plays out in our everyday lives in multiple ways.

In a reading ...

Think about the areas of conflict in your life. Is the fight still worth it? (Was it ever worth it at all?) Consider the way that old battles and grudges can eat up your energy, take up brain space and cause you pain and harm. Might it be time to just walk away – even if that means admitting defeat? Remember that you don't always have to have the last word. It is probably more loving – to yourself and anyone else involved – to admit defeat and turn your attention to something more positive or productive.

And of course, sacrificing this particular fight means you'll have more energy for the bigger picture, or for more meaningful battles.

It can be a helpful card to see when you've lost out in 'battle'. Maybe you came off worst in a difficult breakup, or got fired. This card suggests that no one really won at all, and that you're no more a 'loser' than anyone else.

Still, much may have been lost in this process. If apologies are due, consider it time. If you need to let go and forgive, again, do that work. Don't hang on to old guilt or grievances for the sake of it, and don't scratch at open wounds. Acknowledge that this battle may not be worth fighting any more, and be ready to lay down your sword. Healing may not happen right away – things may be a little raw – but at least there is now space for healing to happen in time.

Six of Swords

Time heals all wounds

This is a restful card, but it is also heavy with thought and emotion. It shows us that process of moving on after a difficult time – tired, but wiser and stronger. Sad, but determined to start over. It's a healing journey.

Many decks show us a person in a boat. They sit, perhaps with their face hidden, facing forwards, away from us. Six swords accompany them in the boat – they are not being left behind. A stranger rows or steers the ship, carrying them to safety. The boat causes no waves, no surf - this journey is slow, its motion is tranquil. In the distance, we see the coast: a new land.

After trauma, conflict, heartbreak, or tough chapters in our lives, we don't have the choice of forgetting everything. We can't simply forget the lessons we learn in life, even when we want to. They stay with us. These experiences may or may not form part of our identities – it may feel empowering to define yourself as, for example, a trauma survivor or a sober alcoholic – or it may feel important *not* to claim your experiences within your current identity. This is a choice you can make. Either way, though, you carry with you the wisdom and lessons of your past lives.

The stranger in the boat may be significant – someone who guides or supports us in our healing. We are not alone in life, this figure may be a real person, or a spiritual helper of any sort. Or, they may be time itself, whose slow, inevitable passage heals wounds and moves us forwards.

The boat itself is significant, too: it travels over water. Whilst this is a Swords card and thus concerned with our minds, there is an emotional journey happening, too. To cross a body of water is symbolically to move forwards, emotionally. There is a quiet, supportive sense of empowerment in this card.

In a reading ...

In its simplest sense, the Six of Swords advises you to begin or continue the process of moving on. This may be easier said than done, but accepting and embracing your own healing journey is the core message of this card.

Healing is transformational. Experiences that may once have been painful or buried deep gradually become a part of your life that you can learn from. Part of who you are, but not you. They are with you, not of you.

It is time for healing to take place, or perhaps it is well underway. You're moving on. You've seen some tough times – perhaps recently, perhaps long ago – and are moving beyond them. You won't forget what you've seen, but will learn to lean on these lessons in the next chapter.

Allow yourself to be helped and supported if you need to. You don't have to do this alone. The Six of Swords can advise counselling and other forms of therapy - anything that helps you to turn experiences into lessons.

Know that there is no need to rush this process. Trust that it is happening.

Seven of Swords

What we hold back

There are many reasons why people might lie, or hide the truth. You may be afraid to be yourself. It may not be safe to tell the whole truth. The Seven of Swords is about what you – or someone else – is/are hiding or holding back, and asks you to consider why.

This card can be about straight-up dishonesty or theft. Underhand tactics or sneaky behaviour. It shines a light on areas of our lives where dishonesty is present, asking us to confront them, to deal with whatever is going on.

Or, it's acknowledgement of our reasons. It wants us to be honest, but it also points to the many reasons a person may not feel able to tell their whole truth. When we see this card in our readings, we are being encouraged to look at these situations and own them as, on some level, dishonest.

In a reading ...

If there is an area of your life where you are not being completely honest, spend some time thinking about this, thinking about what's going on. Is it time to come clean? Maybe, maybe not – explore your feelings around this.

Coming out, or rather, remaining in the closet, is a good example of this. It may be that a person has genuine reason to maintain the illusion of being straight, perhaps with family or at work. If it's not safe for you to come out or reveal your truth, then there is no pressure here to do so. However, if when digging in to this situation you begin to feel it may be time to come out, then the Seven of Swords supports and encourages this decision.

Tone policing is another possible interpretation of this card. There are many reasons why, for example, a Black woman may feel safer playing down her anger, or making conversations about race more comfortable for white people. Patriarchy and white supremacy create codes and norms, continually policing the ways people express experiences, and often punishing voices that challenge the status quo. Often it seems (or is) safer to pretend. If you find you are tone-policing yourself, dig into why this is, explore the price and real meaning of that 'safety'. And know that the problem does not lie with you.

If you feel someone is not being honest with you, then the Seven of Swords says it is time to confront this. That may mean straight-up asking someone what's going on. Or it might look more like walking away, for example, if someone has repeatedly lied to you or hurt you with their dishonesty. Feel your way into this, and decide what is the right approach for you. If you wish to stay in this relationship, how can you create more honesty?

Eight of Swords

Self-doubt

As we've seen in many of the Swords cards, the mind can play tricks on us. In the Eight of Swords, we see one of the most harmful consequences of this: immobilising insecurity.

A little like the Devil, this card gives us a picture of bondage. A figure with their hands tied, blindfolded, surrounded by sharp swords. It's a difficult picture to see.

Especially when we realise that each of those swords represents a thought, a fear, an insecurity. This wall of sharp blades does not really exist – it is a very vivid figment of our mind.

There are so many reasons our minds may create these boundaries, these walls, why we hem ourselves in in these ways. Hard times can teach us to stay small, or lead us to doubt our choices, our own minds. The person on this card feels as though they are a prisoner – unable to move forward or get free of the clutches of self-doubt. But the Eight of Swords holds a mirror to these delusions and encourages us to get free.

In a reading ...

Though this is a caring card, its message can be a tough one, and it is focused on showing you that you have choices. You are not as trapped as you feel, there are options open to you. It can be hard, uncomfortable work to step out of a position of fear or powerlessness, but this is about you taking hold of something you're afraid of. Reframing your situation so that you see options, not barriers. Ultimately, it's empowering — this card wants to hand your power back to you.

When you see this card, ask yourself what unnecessary boundaries are you creating around yourself. Where are you holding back out of fear or self-doubt? Where are you saying, 'I can't ...', when you know you'd really like to try? Challenge yourself to overcome fear and step up to the challenge.

This card can also point to anxiety and/or depression, or other mental health struggles. It can suggest that you or someone else has become trapped by your/their own mind, and could use some support to overcome this. The Eight of Swords doesn't make light of mental health, but points to areas where you can bring in supportive, healing practices or people to help move you forwards.

It also points to self-harm, addiction and self-destructive behaviours – again, a little like the Devil. Remember that you hold the key to your own healing, and that the journey home begins with choosing freedom.

Nine of Swords

Anxiety

Everybody is familiar with that horrible feeling that comes only in the middle of the night. You're the only person awake. And you're filled with an overwhelming sense of fear or dread, so much that you can't sleep. There may be something specific on your mind, or it may be an indefinable anxious feeling – either way, it's got you lying awake, feeling terribly alone.

Though the Nine of Swords may or may not be taking place at midnight, it's a card for being overwhelmed with worry or fear. Like the Eight of Swords, it can point to anxiety – especially the kind where things feel far worse than they really are.

The Nine of Swords can also point to any pressing worry, anything nagging on our minds. Maybe you've put off doing something important and it's about to catch up with you. Maybe you said something you shouldn't have and can't stop thinking about it. This card represents the way it feels when your head gets 'taken over' by worrisome or anxious thoughts — whether big or small, long term or temporary, anxiety is an unpleasant experience.

In a reading ...

So what to do?

This is a very personal card. We all have our ways of dealing with anxiety and there are no rights or wrongs here — the ideas below are simply suggestions.

Rather than prescribing any particular course of action, the Nine of Swords simply encourages you to be kind with yourself, and to find a compassionate perspective.

If you're experiencing actual anxiety, take it seriously. Go gently with yourself, be kind and compassionate to yourself, read up on helpful self-care techniques, do the things that you know will help ease your mind. Get support, if you can. Let folks know where you're at and that you're having a tough time. Don't judge yourself harshly but acknowledge what is happening.

If your experience is more at the 'worry' end of the spectrum, you might focus on practical ways to alleviate your mind. Sometimes writing a to-do list, or starting the very first thing, can be a really helpful way to feel like you're gaining control. Sometimes delegation is the right next step, or asking for help. Or putting down a project entirely.

If you find yourself going over something hurtful in your mind, try to let it rest. Acknowledge the way your mind is being 'taken over' by this event, and allow yourself to reframe it or put it down entirely. Maybe writing a letter will help (even if you never send it), or doing some simple ritual or creative practice to help you let this thing go.

Ten of Swords

Rock bottom is a springboard

The final card in the Swords sequence, the Ten is a bleak sight. No matter the deck, this card shows us a scene of devastation, darkness, woe. Ten swords is a lot to bear, and this suit has been a heavy and difficult one.

This is what rock bottom looks like – all hope seems to be gone.

Except ... it's not. Hope is on the horizon, in the form of the sunrise. A new day will soon begin, and from here there is nowhere to go but up. Be with your feelings, yes, but know also it will soon be time to stand up, dust yourself off, and embrace the dawn.

In this way the Ten of Swords can sometimes (though not always) represent melodrama. Sometimes things just really are the worst – immense grief or pain takes over our lives. Other times, though, there is a light at the end, and a positive, can-do kind of attitude is needed to get past this bump in the road. The Ten of Swords can even be a humorous card. It can be a prod that says 'okay, yes, things feel shitty. But that's about to change.'

This card is a 'ten', and so, is about endings. The closure of an especially tough chapter in your life, one that may have been dominated by your mind, by any or many of the issues we've dealt with in the challenging suit of swords.

In a reading ...

If you're having a tough time right now, know that this is a moment in life, like every other, it will pass. You will get through this. Be with how you feel, acknowledge that you are finding this hard. It's okay. The Ten of Wands can simply be a witness to this moment.

However, if you're feeling very 'woe is me' about something smaller, consider the role your mental attitude is playing in all of this. Are things really as bad as all that? Is there really no way forwards? Is it possible to downsize this issue a little, make it more manageable? Dig deep for the energy to stand up and take action, to overcome your feelings of despair and find positive routes forwards. If appropriate, look for humour.

This card encourages pattern disruption. What might you do to challenge habits that hold you back, how can you create change in your life? Be ready to start over, with a different kind of energy. A little less logical perhaps, and a little more embodied. You'll know yourself where you're going when the time comes. For now, know that a chapter is ending, the wheel is turning, and change is on its way.

The Suit of Wands

The suit of Wands is filled with fire. Burning, brilliant, bright hot fire that moves and transforms and destroys.

In these cards, we get to know the fire that burns inside ourselves. The bright spark of inspiration, the kindling flames of figuring out our paths. The burning energy that comes with the manifestation of the things we want, with passion and drive. It's a life force. It's what makes us who we are.

We find the ego in the Wands suit. Battle, conflict, achievement, status, power – we see what confidence can look like in positive and negative forms, and we see the necessary, humbling lessons that falling from grace can teach.

Fire is a force of creation, but also destruction. Too much fire and we risk losing everything. There is burnout and loss here, too.

But mostly, the Wands are dynamic. It's where we make things happen. We act on our ideas, we work magic. A Wand is a match to light the fire, a torch to light the way. This is a suit of becoming.

Ace of Wands

Inspiration

Regardless of what may come after, this Ace is a beginning. It's a spark. It may come in the form of an idea, a sudden urge to do something, create something, say something. It is the feeling of being gripped by an exciting obsession, the sudden recognition of opportunity. This is a 'yes' card, a 'let's do it' card.

The best ideas are those that are aligned with our values and beliefs. The best ideas are those we can really get behind, those we are prepared to make happen. The best ideas are born from passion, from positive obsession.

> *Prodigy is, at its essence, adaptability and persistent, positive obsession. Without persistence, what remains is an enthusiasm of the moment. Without adaptability, what remains may be channelled into destructive fanaticism. Without positive obsession, there is nothing at all.*

> *Earthseed: The Books of the Living*

> Octavia Butler, *Parable of the Sower*

Having brilliant ideas is one thing, but it's another to put in the work that it takes to bring it to fruition, to create change. Fire alone is inspiring and energising, but to be useful, it must be controlled, used as you need it, directed with intention. As Butler teaches, to be useful, our ideas must be brought to life. We must direct our energy in line with our positive obsessions, willing to adapt, willing to push forth. The journey we find in the Wands suit is at times challenging, rewarding and exhausting. This card is about feeling the fire and signing up to that journey.

Be prepared for this work. Know that your ego will get in the way and commit to being conscious of that. Know that the work will be worth it. For now, feel the heat of your idea and welcome it into your life.

Two of Wands

Preparation is everything

You've got your idea and you're all ready to act ... and the Two of Wands brings you up short. Why? Because the best ideas usually need a little planning.

That's what this card is all about. Being very still with your idea. Letting it ebb and flow in your mind and in your gut. Feel through it. All the elements are present in this card: the fire of the idea, the air of your intellect, your planning mind, the water of your feelings, and the earth of your body's response.

I like to read this card within the sequence: Ace, Two then Three of Wands. Idea, preparation, then action. The Three tells us that it's time to act, but the Two urges us to pause first, and figure out where we're going, what we are trying to achieve. Think of the Chariot's sacred focus. The Magician's conscious intention. That's very present in this card – the Two of Wands shows us the necessary work that comes before forward movement, where take time to get in alignment with our intentions, where we do a little planning.

The duality here (for this is a Two) is that tension between excitement and inaction. Action and stillness. You're preparing to act and there's energy building up inside you, but for now it's better to be still with it. The Two of Wands can have a frustrating 'stuck' feeling to it. Resist the urge to act too soon.

In a reading ...

You stand at a gateway. You are preparing. The time to act is soon. Think of this moment as holding back your bow to shoot an arrow. There is a huge amount of energy held in that bow. It is not yet time to release it – first, take the time to take aim, so you will be able to shoot in confidence.

Take the time to get really clear on where you want to go. This is a good time to write a manifesto, or an action plan, or to speak your intention or your goal aloud. Figure out why you want to do a thing, really understand what it is that's driving you. Connect to the sources of passion inherent in your idea, and work from there.

Feel the ebb and flow of your idea within you. Let it shift – your initial vision may differ greatly from what you finally decide on. Allow space for this to happen. Don't be too quick to act, but explore your idea from different angles, or talk it over with someone.

Feel that tension in you, that feeling of power and potential. You can do something really great here. Know that you have what it takes. Get ready.

This card may also signal returning to an idea you had abandoned long ago. Pick your idea back up and toy with it a while. How does it feel now? Is it time to give it another go?

Three of Wands

Stepping into the unknown

After the stillness and the strategising of the Two, we are ready. It's time to launch that ship, to set sail. It's time to press go.

There is so much magic in manifestation. So much alchemy. The Three of Wands is a reminder of that power. It's a card for sorcery, witchcraft, spellwork. For calling on higher powers, stating intentions, and most importantly, working with the power of your own will. Think of this card as the Minor Arcana version of the Magician. It is about becoming ready, stepping forward into the unknown.

It's not only about beginnings. Threes are often midpoints, turning points, moments of change – here, that could mean a renewed zest for an ongoing project, or pushing through an important decision, or stepping up to new responsibilities.

In a reading ...

Whatever the context, the Three of Wands is about action. Know that you've done the necessary preparation, and you're ready to go.

This is a good time to begin — but it's also a point of achievement in its own right. Feel good and optimistic about your plans, know that you have the strength to do this thing, to see it through. If you're feeling self-doubt, or feeling unprepared, look to sources of encouragement.

Work with your spiritual practices here. State your intentions clearly to the Universe and ask it for help. Call in your intuition. You might want to make a magic wand!

Know that everything is connected and that your actions are an exchange of energy between you and the whole world. Find ways to honour that connection as you move into action.

Four of Wands

A pause and a celebration

This card is another midpoint. We are somewhere along in our journey, and the going has been hard, but good. It's time for a party!

To work and work without feeling real joy and purpose is a depressing thing. The Four of Wands represents work/life balance, a feeling of our projects being part of a wider expression of who we are. We are not only our work, our ideas, the things we create. We are much more than that. This card celebrates that and encourages you to do things that feel good. We are sustained by this kind of balance, nurtured by doing things just for the sheer fun of them, better able to do our more 'serious' work.

The Four of Wands shows us a celebration. It's a 'why not?' card that wants us to stand back and look how far we've come. Sure, there's plenty of work ahead, but now is a good time for a pause.

In a reading ...

Take a moment here. Look at what you've done so far, the way your journey is going. Consider recent achievements, milestones, things you're proud of – these may be big or very small, but it is all worth celebrating.

This is a little like standing on a bridge. From the apex, we can look back at the road so far and forward to the journey ahead. Take a moment. Admire the view. You can work again tomorrow.

As this is a Four, it's also in some ways about structure. Here, that looks like structuring time off into your work schedule, or remembering to share your achievements with friends. This simple act brings joy into our lives, which sustains us in the long run.

The Four of Wands can suggest just about any kind of party. Regardless of your 'journey', maybe it's just time to be playful, have some friends round, or go out on the town. Take this card as permission to have some fun, and acknowledge this as a source of real sustenance.

Five of Wands

A playground tussle

This is a card of conflict, but it is the smaller, less heart-wrenching kind than we see in some cards.

The Five of Wands shows us a battle of egos, people fighting to find out who is strongest. It's the kind of fight you see in a playground, kids working out who is top dog and who will be bottom through fighting or football or handstands, or whatever.

These battles may feel incredibly important in the moment, their outcomes setting a course. But the Five of Wands points out that these egotistic, hierarchical battles are really quite meaningless. It's important to stand up for what we believe in ... but is that really what we're fighting for here?

In a reading ...

You might be feeling really challenged right now – maybe someone is attacking you or calling your beliefs or actions into question. Before you rush to stand up for yourself, consider if it's worth it. What is this battle about, is it really worth fighting? (There are strong echoes here of the Five of Swords).

It may be, of course. So, if you need to fight, avoid pettiness. Don't stoop to dirty tactics and stick with what you know. Stay true to your principles. Don't be drawn in to someone else's war of egos – some battles are not yours to fight, others are simply not worth engaging in.

The Five of Wands might be pointing to any area of conflict in your life. If so, try to take a common-sense approach to the situation. Rein in the urge to just attack on all sides, and figure out what's really going on. And again, ask yourself – is this worth my time and energy?

Six of Wands

Victory and humility

The Six of Wands offers us a picture of victory. Something has worked out well, and this is a time to feel proud. There are plenty of parallels with the Four of Wands here, though whilst that card is about the energy of celebration itself, the Six is focused on the experience of triumph.

Following a card of conflict (the Five of Wands) the Six may refer to triumph in some kind of battle – 'winning' anything from a minor disagreement to a political or legal battle. When this does refer to situations of conflict, though, it carries a reminder that the battle is not the war. This current triumph does not solve – or resolve – everything. It is a step on a path.

But of course, this doesn't have to be about 'battles' and 'wars'. We don't need miliatary language to understand the concept of victory. The moment of triumph we see in the Six of Wands can take many forms. In the Wild Unknown Tarot, the card shows a butterfly, rising up from a sea of shadows. This can be about spreading our wings and feeling free, rising above what we were previously fighting. It's a moment of becoming, of personal celebration, overcoming old battles, especially battles with ourselves.

In a reading ...

This is a good sign for any situation in which you're fighting for what you believe in. It's a sign of strength, courage, and righteousness.

Beyond fighting, though, take this card as encouragement to be true to yourself and stand up for what you feel is right. Honour your principles. 'Be on the right side of history'. Put personal gain aside and focus your energy on the good of the whole, the community.

This card can also indicate leadership – a moment for you to really step up. If you really believe in your principles, there is nothing to fear here. Be bold and fair; lead this part of the journey.

Implicit in this card of 'victory' is of course the advice to stay humble. These moments of confidence and celebration are wonderful and can be enjoyed, of course. Know that this is not an ending, that the journey continues, and there is work still to do. Some may put it more bluntly: pride comes before a fall. I don't feel that a 'fall' is implicit in this card, but it does carry encouragement to remember where you came from.

A good way to do this is to acknowledge your lineage, to give gratitude, and to pay it forwards. Nobody achieves great things purely on their own. Look back and acknowledge the people and circumstances that enabled you to reach this point of success – friends, colleagues, strangers, family, inherited privilege, and anyone who you may have stepped on (intentionally or not) on the road so far. Own all of this, acknowledge their part in your story, and be grateful and humble. Then ask — how can I use this moment to open doors for others?

Seven of Wands

Never mind the haters

We've talked a lot about 'battles' in the Wands suit – because life can sometimes feel like a fight. We are called on all the time to speak out, to stand up for ourselves, to overcome this inner voice or that external force of oppression.

The Seven of Wands is an activist's card. It's that image that shows up to say, 'Your truth belongs to you. Hold it high.' For some of us this may be an actual fight for survival in a society that won't accept our existence. For others, it is about standing tall and getting our message out there so it can be heard.

In some decks, we see a physical battle. A person standing alone, their single wand held high, fighting a sea of faceless others. This is how it can feel sometimes, when we are called to defend our truths. Other decks represent it differently. Charissa Drengsen's Steampunk Tarot shows women gossiping about another from behind parasols. The Wild Unknown Tarot shows a single, burning flame, casting other wands into the dark.

All of these are images of empowerment for the 'lonely' one, the 'other'. They celebrate otherness and critique the 'haters' that threaten it. The Seven of Wands recognises marginal truths, the lived experiences and stories that don't get heard in the mainstream. It asks each of us to be proud of who we are, to own our truths and our experiences and it bears witness to the ways this can feel like a fight to be seen or to survive.

It's important to feel the joy in this card, even though it is again one of conflict. At its heart, it celebrates your power, your light, your difference. It wants that light to shine, bold and bright, for all to see. It celebrates who you are, and reminds you that you are powerful and can create change.

In a reading ...

A little like the Five of Wands, you may feel really attacked right now, or called to stand up for yourself. Unlike that card, however, here the fight is worth it. The Seven of Wands seeks to embolden you and remind you that you are strong, powerful, brilliant.

As an activist's card, this points to any situation where you have to stand up for your beliefs. This includes standing up for others. If you enjoy power and privilege, use that strength to lift others, or offer space on your platform for others to step up and join you. There is a loneliness in this card because it is focused on your power and difference as an individual, but within this is the question of what you can do with that power. Focus on that. Resist the ego's urge to stay in that space of individualism. Find your people, surround yourself with folks who 'get it' so you and others are not isolated.

Regardless of the presence of a 'real' fight, this is about celebrating who you are and being unafraid to show it. We live in a society that prizes conformity, that offers us very narrow ideas of what a 'good' or 'successful' person looks like. Many of us are left out of those spaces the very moment we are conceived. Others move through life, gradually realising that this mould is not for them. Be proud of what makes you different, what makes you you. Don't hide it away, but bring it forth to make the world more beautiful, more colourful. And, ultimately, to ensure that you yourself are free.

Eight of Wands

Deliver your message

This is a dynamic, forward moving card. Something is in motion, something is on its way. Something may have even arrived.

The Eight of Wands is about messages. Loud, direct messages. Not secret signs, not 'maybe's, but clear communications with purpose and meaning. This is where our ideas get spoken into the world. Shouted into the world. Passed on. There is a gathering of momentum here that comes from the right words, spoken at the right time.

In a reading ...

Ideas are infectious. If you've got something worth saying, find a way to share it. Be clear and direct, don't mess about with fluff. Be strategic. How can you make your ideas easy for others to hear and understand? How can you speak so that those who need to get the message will get it?

Think carefully about communication, especially the way that you communicate. Think beyond common interpretations of 'communication', too, and consider other forms of passing on messages, such as your body language, the way you show up (or don't), everything about yourself that conveys something about who you are, what you're about.

It may just be that there's something you want to say – to the world, to just one person, to yourself. Give that message the time and energy it deserves.

Take care over it. Try to get it right, don't rush or be clumsy. Respect and honour the power in your words to affect others and change the world.

Nine of Wands

It's worth it

The Nine of Wands shows us the flip side of the Wands' dynamic, exciting action: tiredness. Energy comes in limited supplies, and there are times when we all feel like giving up.

This card is about that moment. It's a recognition of weariness that necessarily comes after periods of intense work. Maybe you've been working on a creative project for what feels like forever. Maybe you're sick and tired of fighting for your rights. Maybe you're wondering if that thing that once seemed so precious and important is really worth this much energy.

This card is essentially about keeping on. It brings a reminder: this is worth it. You are worth it.

The suit of Wands teaches us that our best work comes forth form a place of real passion deep inside us. That fire in our bellies in which great ideas are formed. Those positive obsessions. We birth these ideas and turn them into action, we create, we push forwards, we bring all kinds of wonderful things into the world, we shape change.

But heck, does it take some effort. And if you're feeling tired just now? That's okay.

In the Wild Unknown Tarot, Kim Krans illustrates the Nine of Wands as a steep ladder or mountain of wands. It looks hard. It looks tough. At the top shines a crescent moon, because this is soul work. What you're doing is meaningful. This isn't just about material accomplishments or a moment of fame – the work you're doing is teaching you something about who you are, and it is making the world a better place.

Each of those wands is a big and perhaps difficult step. You have taken many, and there are more to come. Rest, of course, if you need to. But don't give up.

In a reading ...

If you're at the start of something, this card wisely reminds you that the going will get tough at times. Every project has ups and downs built in, from the moment you get fired up and press 'go' to the moment you just want to give up and pack it all in. If you really believe in this thing, you have to be prepared to go through those low points, too. You have to keep the faith.

There's a celebration built into this moment, in that it's a 'nearly there' card – all Nines carry within themselves the knowledge that the Ten, completion, is just around the corner. In that way, there is a voice here saying, 'One last push! You're so close! You can do it!'

On the other hand, maybe you're starting to believe that this isn't 'soul work' after all. Maybe you've changed, your priorities have changed, you just don't believe in that same goal any more? Depending on other cards in your reading, the Nine of Wands may be encouraging you to get back to the principles at the heart of your work and check that you still truly believe in what you do. If that passion really isn't there, it's time to make a change.

Ten of Wands

You are not your achievements

We've all done it. We've all said 'yes' so many times that, before we know it, we're drowning in duties and promises and to-do lists.

We meant well, of course. We wanted to help, or move something forward, or feel useful, or wanted. Or else we just had to get this stuff done because it's our damn job.

But, as we saw in the Nine of Wands, we all have our capacity. We all have our limits. There are moments in life where our to-do lists simply become too much.

In the Rider-Waite-Smith version of this card, a person staggers forwards. The way they are holding their ten wands is quite ridiculous, spread out like a fan in front of their face. They can't possibly see where they are going, all they can see is this great load of projects, ideas, actions, obligations, or whatever else these wands represent. Surely it would be better to put a few of those wands down? Carry them one or two at a time, perhaps?

It's a shame that the Wands suit – so filled with passion and dynamic energy – should end up here at this place of overwhelm. In this, it represents our immaturity with the element of fire. Fire is such a powerful force. As we've seen throughout this suit, it can rile us up, get us so excited about our ideals and our ideas, it can bring about positive action, it can encourage us to fight for what we truly believe in. But, of course, we can have too much of a good thing. And fire left unchecked can be all-consuming.

That's what's happened here. We have taken on more than we can handle, and the result is that we get lost or burned out.

In a reading ...

You're overwhelmed. With so much on your plate, it's hard to know where on earth to focus your energy, or how on earth you're going to get all of this done.

One answer is to let go of control and let someone help you. Remember that Wands very often point to ego, and our egos are so often bound up in our achievements. Our ability to tick things off a list and pronounce our days 'productive'. It's time to let go of that need. You are not the sum of your achievements, your worth is not measured by a fully-crossed-off list.

You do not have to do All Of The Things. Did someone tell you you did? It is time to learn the delicate yet vital survival skill of saying 'no'.

People with disabilities or chronic illness talk of Spoon Theory — the idea that we each begin each day with a certain number of 'spoons' of energy, those without disability or chronic illness having more spoons, those with having fewer, and so having to choose more carefully how they will be used.[10] If this reflects your own experience and you are living with disability, chronic illness and limited spoons, the Ten of Wands offers encouragement to be gentle; permission to give yourself rest, to flake or change your mind (and to not beat yourself up about it.)

There is a message in this card for activists. So focused on what we are doing

---

[10] The Spoon Theory, a personal story and analogy of what it is like to live with sickness or disability, by Christine Miserandino. See butyoudontlooksick.com/articles/written-by-christine/the-spoon-theory.

for the struggle, we may forget to take care of our own needs. The Ten of Wands is a reminder that the sustainability of our movements comes from carefully building self-care into our practices. (What use is a group that fights for people's rights if all of its volunteers are burned out?)

Whether you feel like this right now, or if you feel just fine and not tired at all — think about *capacity*. It's a sum, a number, a thing that has an actual limit. Think about the ways you waste energy ('busy work', for example) and how this can diminish your capacity for more important things.

The Suit of Cups

The suit of Cups is the realm of water. Remember how water appears as such a strong symbol in the Major Arcana? It represents feelings, emotion, intuition and spirituality. The unconscious. Think of the different ways water exists in nature - a raging, stormy sea, a wide river slowly carving its path, the glassy calmness of a still lake, the excitement of a tumbling waterfall, a massive iceberg, a morning mist ... and you begin to get a picture of the fluid, shifting, unpredictable nature of this element.

Tarot's Cups are metaphorical 'containers' for all those things. In this suit, we explore how the intangible element of water manifests in our lives – through love, personal development, spirituality, sadness, kindness, vulnerability, and more.

Here, we'll see relationships blossom and bloom. We celebrate friendship, we open our hearts to others. This is a story of growth towards genuine, deeply felt fulfilment, coming home to ourselves. Feeling at home within ourselves. The suit of Cups recognises vulnerability as a strength, a source of power. This kind of growth is not a linear process, we'll also see loss and pain, letting go, and determination to move forwards and explore new inner landscapes.

The suit of Cups is one for inner work, for challenging ourselves and showing up for the necessary work of looking into our own hearts and souls, and working with the longing and desire that live there.

Ace of Cups

The open heart

All of tarot's Aces bring new starts. Opportunities. Each Ace holds out an offering – it is up to you to reach forward and take it. Here in the suit of Cups, this is an opportunity for spiritual and emotional growth.

This card heralds a new chapter in your inner life. You may feel called to do some kind of spiritual work or study. To take up a new magical practice, or dive deeper into your faith, whatever shape that may take.

When you see this card, listen to your heart. It's a cliché, but it's about deepening into personal work. Your heart is in many ways wiser than your mind, it knows things, truths, that are not rational or easily explained. It's time to give those truths some time and space, to honour that wisdom you hold deep within you, to really listen.

The Ace of Cups is also about falling in love. This is a profound and beautiful life event that can take many forms, from romantic love to self-love to deep connections with other special people in our lives. You can fall in love with a friend. You can fall in love with a practice. You can fall in love with a place, an animal, a work of art.

This card is an invitation to *open* your heart and let that love flow in. It requires you to be vulnerable. Listen to what your heart is telling you, what it wants. Don't worry about what is 'acceptable' or what 'fits', just pay attention to the desire and longing you feel inside.

The Ace of Cups wants you to embrace who you are and live authentically, with integrity and self-respect. It represents a new opportunity to do just that.

Two of Cups

Vulnerability as strength

This is what it looks like to be generous and vulnerable. This is how it feels to open up your heart and offer its contents to another. To give of yourself, and to receive, too.

The Two of Cups is an exchange. You offer your cup – a container for all the love and pain and mystery in your heart – to someone, to something. In return, you receive their cup. There is so much trust here, so much willingness to be naked in this way.

Though falling in love is not the only interpretation of this card, it's a good metaphor for its message. Falling in love is a risk — saying 'I love you' is riskier still. How often do we hold back what we really feel for fear of rejection, or ridicule, or simply not fitting in? How often do we push down what we really feel, unable to accept our own desires?

The Two of Cups is the opposite. Feeling the fear, maybe, but reaching out all the same. Saying yes, I'm up for this. I'll show you my heart, if you show me yours. These are the few tentative and bold first steps into a new relationship built on love and trust.

In a reading ...

If you have a partner, this card may be pointing to that relationship. If you have multiple lovers, it points to your relationship with one person in particular. The number two here is important – this is about an intimate exchange between two people. It's about that bond of love or friendship or family that enables us to be truly open and comfortable with someone else.

Beyond people, this card also represents the trust in our relationship to other things – a practice, a role, or a place. The Ace of Cups shows an opportunity to take a new spiritual path, to listen to your heart and follow its desires. The Two shows us what it looks like to take that opportunity, to take those first steps. It requires courage. You may be falling in love with yourself. You may be entering into a new spiritual practice that asks you to be vulnerable, to make an offering. You may be making any kind of commitment based on love and trust.

In all cases, this card highlights the trust that is necessary for this to happen. Be vulnerable. Be truthful. Express yourself. Be generous with your emotions and remember that wonderful rule of give and take: you receive from the Universe what you are prepared to offer it. Give freely of yourself, understanding that this an act of beautiful and profound exchange.

Three of Cups

Joy and connection

This is a card of celebration. It's the energy of good friends, who love each other unconditionally, sharing a moment of sheer joy. Times are good when we have each other. The essence of this card is one of friendship, and a feeling that together with our friends, we have all that we need. We give, we receive, we are held, supported, loved for who we are.

It's a gang, or the outcasts at school. It's a team of businesswomen who lift each other up. It's your childhood friends, who know you better than anyone. It's an activist group, basing their actions in love and mutual support, knowing that they are stronger together. Or it might just be a really great party.

In a reading ...

The Three of Cups suggests good times. Happy, free, sociable times. It's a lovely card to see in our readings, for it says 'you are loved'.

Celebrate your friends. Reach out to them, tell them how much you love them. Make time to hang out, throw a party, go on a day trip, call round for a cuppa. Think about how much your friends – or a friend – means to you, and let them know. Remind yourself how much strength and energy there is in being part of a community of friends – three is the magic number, and there's magic here. You give a lot, you get a lot back – again, there's an exchange.

It may be time to ask for support from your community, or to give back. If times are hard for you, reach out and ask for the love and support you need. Or if someone you know needs help, now is the time to be a good friend. What can you offer? How can you be of service?

For some this card may point to polyamory or the opening up of a two-person relationship. Welcoming in a new person, bringing in new dynamics. As this is the suit of Cups, we're firmly in the feelings zone here – remember to check in with your heart regularly, and with the hearts of others. In polyamorous relationships there is an emphasis on heartfelt and honest communication.

In the suit of Pentacles, the Three indicates teamwork. It's similar here, but the focus is less on specific roles and achievements and 'work', and more on the energy of mutual support. If you're struggling in a group situation just now, try to put aside a need for self-advancement, quiet that nagging urge for fame or recognition. Know that you are part of something bigger. Focus on all the strength and skills you have in your group, and to share positive energy. Focus on lifting each other up and strengthening the group as a whole.

Four of Cups

Apathy

Sometimes, you just feel stuck. Not because of obstacles, not for any practical reason that can be solved, but just ... stuck. It's like your heart gives up, you can't seem to get going or get excited about things.

The Four of Cups is about that moment. It represents an emotional inertia, grinding to a standstill. It's being apathetic (as in, 'without feeling'), or stuck in denial. It can represent a 'hater' mentality - getting mired in critique and negativity, rather than looking for alternative ways forwards.

In Pamela Colman Smith's illustration, a girl sits beneath a tree looking fed up. Three cups sit before her. Apparently, she is not interested in what is in them. She has become bored. Bored with her own heart. Bored with herself.

It's a rut, for sure, but it is a momentary one. A lapse in imagination, a lack of curiosity. From the side of Colman Smith's picture a fourth cup is offered, as if by magic. Looking just like a miniature version of the Ace of Cups, this fourth cup is another opportunity, something new. She only has to turn her head to see it – but will she?

In a reading ...

Apathy and denial are seductive. What are you refusing to engage with, or choosing not to accept? Whilst stillness and slowness can be great teachers (as in the Hanged Man or Two of Wands), here things have become stale. You now face a choice. You can sit there being grumpy or bored and allow yourself to get bogged down in your apathy or denial. Or, you can make a change. When you see this card, it's up to you.

How might you make such a change? It needn't be about huge gestures - it's more about shifting your perspective. Adopt an attitude of curiosity. Let your imagination wander. Try something new. Be creative – literally, get out some paints or make a collage, or whatever. Wander the streets, hug a tree, or go to the beach. You get the idea! It's up to you to give things a shake and awaken your imagination – by doing so, you open up new perspectives and possibilities that can help you get back on track again.

This might point to a relationship becoming stale, losing interest in something or someone you once loved. This can be painful and hard to face - it's so common to live with denial for a long time before acceptance, before change. In these times, the Four of Cups is a gentle nudge - it makes no demands, but asks you to be honest about what's going on, and how you're responding.

This card is also about gratitude. Under capitalism, we are taught to focus on lack, on what we don't have, on our 'not-enough-ness'. The Four of Cups is a prompt to shift our focus to the riches and gifts of our lives, encouraging us to cultivate a sense of abundance and possibility.

On the other hand, the Four of Cups may also be about saying 'no' or refusing action for positive reasons. Maybe the 'right' person hasn't come along yet. Maybe it's wise to hold out for a better offer. There's a passivity in this card that could be just what you need right now, if you have faith that something better is just around the corner. Just take care not to get stuck here in the waiting.

Five of Cups

Permission to grieve

The Five of Cups shows us a moment of pure sadness. In the Rider-Waite-Smith tarot, there's little here but a lone figure, standing sadly beside overturned cups.

What happened? It doesn't really matter. Whatever those cups held is now gone, and this person is left to deal with it.

Though actually, this isn't about 'dealing' with things. It's about letting those feelings happen. Loss is painful. Breakups are painful. Life hurts. It's okay to feel sad: the Five of Cups offers us all permission to grieve, to sit in the sadness we feel for whatever reason, to feel it all through.

In many illustrations of this card, two cups remain upright. They represent hope, and all of the positive, wonderful energy in the Two of Cups. Right now they are untouched, ignored. Hope is there in the background for when we are ready. For the moment, it's okay to simply sit with the loss and feel our own pain.

In a reading ...

Let yourself be sad. If you're putting on a brave face or being strong for someone else or for yourself, now is the time to drop the act. Really give yourself the space to feel what you feel. It may be simple grief. It may be a complex mix of things. Go with it.

You don't have to *be* anything for anybody. All you must do right now is feel. Healing begins with honesty, with grief – that might take a few days, it may take years, and both are fine.

Remember, though, that life goes on around you. Those two cups – symbols of so much possibility for joy, love and fulfilment – are right behind you. Whenever you are ready, they will be there for you. Hold that knowledge deep inside and let it support you as you work through how you feel just now.

This can also represent going back to an old wound. If there's anything you have 'stuffed down' in the past, a grief, guilt or grudge that you carry, now is a good time to face that. Don't be afraid of it – make some space in your life so that you can gently acknowledge what happened. This is about healing, beginning with being truly honest about how you feel.

Six of Cups

Rooted in kindness

Often it is the simplest things that mean the most. Small gestures of love that remind us someone cares. A word, a smile, a gift. There is so much power in kindness, it is a true force.

The Six of Cups celebrates acts of kindness and generosity. It encourages us to bring more of this into our lives and to focus on what really matters. What use is wealth, nice clothes, a big home, if we can't love each other or share what we have? Meditate on this simple lesson. Look for ways to live a kinder life, encourage others to do the same.

There is a deeper meaning to this card, too – about rootedness and belonging. The Six of Cups raises themes of family and ancestry and where we each come from, specifically in relation to how these things inform your own life now. It asks us to explore what it feels like to be 'rooted' – that may be physically in a space, or it may be in a culture, tradition or lineage of which we are a part.

In a reading ...

When you see this card, look for simple ways to inject a little love and kindness into your situation. Reach out to someone who needs it. Buy yourself some flowers. Send that message of support. Donate.

It's so easy to take our loved ones for granted, to snap at a partner, ignore a friend's text. Don't. Know that these relationships are gifts and require energy to survive. Put that energy in – it needn't be laborious or require much of you. Remember that the simpler things in life are often what matter more. Don't forget to say 'I love you'.

This is also about your roots. Try to connect to a simpler time in your life – perhaps your childhood or a time you felt carefree. What mattered to you then? What were your goals? Where did you find joy, companionship, fun? What was your daily life like?

By the same token, the Six of Cups often points to a person who has got stuck in the past – perhaps acting, talking or seeing things as they did a long time ago. If this is the case, the Six of Cups shines a soft light on that behaviour, bringing encouragement to turn around and look to the future – or, more importantly, the present.

This card brings a warm invitation to explore your roots. The Six of Cups can often be about connecting backwards, with family, grandparents, or perhaps ancestors. Think about the place from which you came, and your relationship to it now. In what ways do you carry forwards your own roots? How do you hear and honour the stories of ancestors you carry? What is the meaning of those stories in your own life?

Perhaps you have torn up your roots and looking backwards in this way is painful or not appropriate for you just now. That's okay. This card imagines yourself rooting into something new. Imagine the healthy, happy roots you would like to create for yourself, and know that these roots will be safe.

Seven of Cups

Depth over breadth

This card is a wild one. Besides what you see on your own version of this card, try an online image search and you'll see what I mean. Treasure, demons, mythical figures ... what on earth is going on here?

This could be about a boundless imagination, and the importance of giving our dreams structure and support. Rachel Pollack puts it best in *Seventy Eight Degrees of Wisdom*:

> *Emotion and imagination can produce wonderful visions, but without grounding in both action and the outer realities of life these fantastic images remain daydreams, 'fancies' without real meaning or value. ... They lack meaning because they don't connect to anything outside of themselves.*

It's good to be imaginative and curious, of course! But ideas, callings, desires, if they aren't acted upon they remain like the symbols in this card: figments of your mind or, rather, your heart. Any of us may have beautiful visions; we give these meaning by following through and really seeing where they can take us, exploring the new emotional and spiritual landscapes we can create if we make brave choices.

There's excitement here, and also fear. What would happen if you really just followed your heart?

In a reading ...

Your ideas may be wonderful, but can you make them real? What can they really mean, here, in your life? The Seven of Cups asks you to 'make the impossible possible', to actively manifest your desires, rather than admiring them as daydreams. In order to put in this energy, you may need to let some dreams go. Let your heart guide you to choose the meaningful over the superficial.

This is about making proactive choices. Perhaps you're faced with too many, and you just can't pick one path. Maybe you want to do All Of The Things. Perhaps you're torn between lovers. Perhaps there are just too many things vying for your attention right now and you're feeling lost or overwhelmed.

Choice can be a burden, and the Seven of Cups opens up a discussion about that kind of spiritual 'weight'. What does it look like to choose something and really go deep with it, rather than dabbling without purpose in many things? This card promotes depth over breadth, and thus asks for commitment.

Eight of Cups

The courage to walk away

This is another 'moving on' card. It's about making the difficult, sad, and ultimately wise choice to leave something behind and forge a new path.

The Eight of Cups is a brave goodbye. We have all experienced moments in our lives when we realise things just aren't working as they are, and that they can't be mended. We have put in care and energy and love, we have worked hard – but it's time to stop trying.

It's the kindest of breakups – the setting free of friends or lovers so they may walk their own paths. The letting go of ties that bind because things have changed. There's so much acceptance and respect here. The Eight of Cups honours goodbyes, honours the strength and wisdom in doing them well.

This is very much an act of self-respect. We must love ourselves enough to change what isn't working, to set ourselves free from the things that hold us back or hurt us. We have to learn to let go of what doesn't serve us, and allow others to do the same. Thus, the Eight of Cups is imbued with a sense of generosity, the putting aside of the needy ego, giving space for healing, growth and change.

In a reading ...

It's time to go. If you're not already on your way, then this card asks you to accept what isn't working in your life – especially those things into which you've poured a lot of energy. Look at what is not sustainable, what is not feeling okay, and give yourself permission to let it go.

Do this with love and respect. Honour the time you have put into this part of your life, think of what was good about it. You can take those good things with you, they are a part of you. Forgive yourself for the mistakes you have made, forgive others where needed.

It may feel right to mark this turning point with a ritual of some kind. A fire, burning old letters, an altar to the future, a divorce party: feel your way through to a ceremony that works for you. Show respect and love to the act of letting go, of making this kind of brave, wise, yes often sad choice. Leave room for grief, knowing that this is part of the process.

And remember that, though this is about the goodbye, it's also about what lies ahead. The road may be long, it will be a healing journey and it may be hard, but it's time to take those first steps. Take with you only what you need, and leave the rest behind.

Nine of Cups

Feeling good

Sometimes, you just want to feel good. Not in any especially profound way, not as a result of a load of hard work or a 'journey', but just good, plain and simple. That's this card.

The Nine of Cups shows us simple satisfaction with what we have. It's number Nine, not Ten, meaning this isn't 'total fulfilment', but it's damn close. Things feel good.

There's a real sense of ease here, a comfort in knowing that things are okay, our needs are met, we are safe. Like the Six of Cups and the Sun, this card reminds us of life's everyday pleasures and encourages us to seek happiness there.

You are enough. You have enough. You are safe.

On the other hand, this card may sometimes be a sign of superficiality – it can point to a tendency to look only at the surface of a situation when beneath things are not so simple or so rosy. Perhaps someone is pretending for some reason, deliberately not seeing the truth.

Traditionally, this is known as the 'wish' card. In divination, it can portend that your wishes will come true. It's image of satisfaction is an auspicious card for anyone who is ready to state their desires.

In a reading ...

Let yourself breathe, feel safe, feel good. Allow yourself to just know that you are okay, and that is enough. That you are enough. Sometimes, the most important thing is just to remember that.

Again: you are enough.

If you've been caught up in chasing after any kind of goal – especially something in your relationships or your spiritual life – Nine of Cups reminds you that you are doing fine and it's okay to let up a little. Pause to enjoy this moment. Things are constantly changing, but now is a good time to stop and be present, to enjoy the things you have right now.

If the above words about superficiality ring a bell for you, the Nine of Cups can be encouraging you to go a little deeper. Don't pretend things are perfect if there's something you need to deal with. Be honest about what's not great in your life, and know that it's okay not to have it all together.

And: make a wish. Name your desires. Ask the Universe for help. This card brings good fortune!

Ten of Cups

Heart's home

This card has been illustrated in many different ways. A group of friends gathered by the sea, feet all together in the water. A happy family with a pretty cottage. A rainbow. A circus. A Pride parade. A ceremonial dinner.

What they have in common is that they are all imbued with a sense of homecoming. This is the final card in the Cups sequence, and it shows us what the complete fulfilment of this suit looks like. Our heart come home. We know who we are, where we are, why we are here (or we are joyfully surrendered to the mystery). We are safe and supported. We have the love that we need.

Home can mean so many things to so many people. As this is a Cups card (rather than Pentacles), we are talking about spiritual home, emotional home, rather than bricks and mortar – though a physical home can definitely be a part of this picture. Home is arriving at a place where we feel happy, where we accept ourselves, where we give and receive love. For some this may be easy to find and manifest, we may even be born into this feeling of security. Others may search long and hard to find chosen family, peace and acceptance.

As a Ten, this shows us the completion of another of life's cycles. It is the closing of a time of heart-focused, deep work so that a new energy can move in. The heart has learned so much and it's now time for a shift to take place.

In a reading ...

The Ten of Cups may appear as a simple celebration. If you're feeling great just now, then this card is another friend, clinking a celebratory glass. It wants you to pause and honour the good things in your life, and really enjoy this moment.

Embrace the people you love. Practice acts of kindness. Reach out. Remember all of the loving acts we've seen in this suit of Cups – the vulnerability, the generosity, the trust – and know that this card is the culmination of all of that, along with the hard things, too; grief and loss, those times of feeling stuck. It's all there. You are strong and brave and you know yourself well. This is a moment to feel really proud and at home in your own life.

What does 'home' mean to you? What does it feel like? Who and what is there? The Ten of Cups is all about your personal vision of fulfilment, and helping you to move towards that vision in your real life. It wants you to be happy! And the first thing to think about is what happiness actually looks like, for you.

This card can point to a person who feels tied to someone else's vision of happiness. Society has many ways of presenting us with 'ideals' – rigid moulds that are not comfortable for everyone. The Ten of Cups then emphasises the need to acknowledge the ways you are coerced into this mould, and to commit to defining your own idea of happiness, ultimately to break free. You cannot be truly fulfilled if you are living someone else's version of your life.

As always with the Tens, know that this is the completion of something, that things are about to change. That doesn't mean everything is about to fall apart! Only that this moment is the culmination of a lot of emotional work. Your heart has been on a huge journey and you've learned so much. Look upon it all and embrace who you are. Be proud.

The Face Cards

The tarot's cast of characters

The 16 Face (or 'court') cards – that is the Pages, Knights, Kings and Queens — *are* part of the Minor Arcana.

They get their own section in this book because they follow their own system within the four suits. They don't so much lead into or follow on from the 'pips' (the Ace-through-Ten cards) – it's more like they show us each suit's energy within the hands of different people.

Of all the cards in the tarot, I find it's these cards that confuse people most.

I find it helpful to think of these cards as representing different 'stages'. This might mean 'life stages', for example the Pages as curious children, the Knights as gung-ho teens or younger adults, the Kings as fully-grown, highly skilled adults, and the Queens as older and wiser figures who understand life on a deep level.

Or these stages may be a person working through any kind of journey. A self-development goal, a community project, an artwork, a course of study – anything that has early stages, a middle, and an end point. Many decks use alternate names for these stages. The Collective Tarot, for example, calls Pages 'Seekers', Knights 'Apprentices', Queens 'Artists' and Kings 'Mentors' (further examples are given below). You can see how these different titles for the cards change the way we might read them.

Each card is a character. They highlight your skills, approaches, mindset, feelings. As such, they *embody* their own meaning in a human way. They represent you — or at least an aspect, a dimension of your self, your humanity. Or instead they may signify other people in your life, and the particular ways they're influencing or impacting you.

Exploring the Face cards

Binary gender

In particular, we find gender-normativity in the Face cards. The association of Queens with inner work and caring, Kings with power and control, and (traditionally male) Knights with action and boldness, for example, all serve to reinforce gendered stereotyping, whilst the expected pronouns of the different cards can throw us off when thinking about the people they represent in our readings.

Whilst some decks feature renamed Face cards (see below), most don't, and the work is on the reader to break away from enforcing gender norms in our tarot practice. One simple way to disrupt gender-normativity when reading these cards is by playing with pronouns – referring to cards with the gender-neutral pronouns 'they/them', or switching up the obvious pronouns so that Queens become 'he' and Kings 'she', as I've done in this book. Some decks, like Cristy C. Road's wonderful Next World Tarot, depict figures of different gender to the expected norm, a beautifully simple, visual way to disrupt gender normativity of tarot tradition.

Renaming the Face cards

Some decks forego the traditional titles of Page, Knight, Queen and King, and use other names to express these different ages. I love and appreciate this kind of reinterpretation of these 16 important cards – leaving behind royal titles allows us to step that little bit further away from an imperial, hierarchical understanding of society, whilst also (often) ditching the gender norms, too. These new titles also offer new keys to interpreting the cards (for example, renaming the traditional Page as 'Student' reminds us of these cards' qualities of curiosity and learning).

A few examples (corresponding to Page / Knight / Queen / King respectively):

- Slow Holler Tarot: Student / Traveller / Visionary / Architect
- World Spirit Tarot: Seer / Seeker / Sybil / Sage
- Thea's Tarot: Child / Amazon / Daughter / Mother

This swapping about can be confusing, especially if you're new to tarot! As always, if your deck uses different titles, I encourage you to grab a pen and write your own card names directly into this book, so you can find and refer to them easily.

Structure and hierarchy

Most decks and books will place the King at the head of each suit, suggesting that each King represents the ultimate level of maturity within that sphere. In my own understanding of these cards, I disagree with that framing, and in this book I have presented the court cards in my preferred order: Page, Knight, King, Queen.

Working with my cards, I've come to feel that the Queen, who deeply internalises the lessons of their suit and uses those lessons to personally grow, represents the true culmination of a suit's story. The King, meanwhile, is adept at using the suit's qualities for external means, in a more social context. This is powerful indeed, but not as powerful or as mature as the Queen.

Of course, in real-life terms, there is no hierarchy here – both expressions are equally valid and important when it comes to building just, stable societies, and we all need to create a balance between our outer and inner lives, our outer and inner work. I call the Queen the 'culmination' because I feel that the Queen's skills of integration and embodiment are the hardest to attain and practice, they require a deeper work than the King's skills of building, power, accumulation.

Page of Pentacles

Joy in exploration

As the child of the Pentacles suit (whether 'child' here means youth, or more likely a childlike attitude,) this person is curious and adventurous, interested in the world around her. She looks carefully at her surroundings, her body, her environment, and asks questions.

This is about taking pleasure in your studies. A fascination with how things work and what they mean, so that you are looking really closely at the elements of your life. You may decide to travel far and wide to gather more experience and information, to learn more.

Explorations befitting the Page of Pentacles include travel, sex, anything in the 'natural world', taking up new crafts and hobbies (especially things with your hands, or sensual experiences), exploring your own body or gender expression, house-hunting, job-hunting, and so on. With this card we take that earthy realm we find in the Pentacles cards, and place it in the hands of someone who is curious.

There is an optimism and a sense of wonder here, as with all the Pages. Open minded, open hearted, you are willing to discover something good, seeking good things. Your mind is not yet made up. It's a very light, very non-attached position, filled with potential, but not set on any specific destination. There's a lot of freedom here.

The Page of Pentacles represents joy in the journey itself. You may have a clear idea where you're going right now, or none at all – either is fine. Focus on enjoying the present moment, really savouring each step, each small discovery. Indulge your senses, stop and smell the roses, be open to finding pleasure in the world around you.

As the Pentacles can sometimes represent work, this card encourages taking pleasure in your hard work. If you are job-hunting right now, try to move towards things you know you will find satisfying if you have the choice. If you're about to start a project of any kind, make sure it's something that will peak your curiosity and feel fulfilling to do.

Special skills

Curiosity, eagerness to travel and explore, adventurousness.

Knight of Pentacles

Dedication

This is a hardworking card. The Knight of Pentacles is someone who knows that the road ahead is long, and quietly gets on with it.

The energy here is steady, perhaps slow. It's about facing each challenge as it comes up, practice and diligence, being prepared to fall off – and then climb back upon – the horse, perhaps many times. This is a person you can rely on to see things through, the friend that may not be the most fun at parties, but who you know you can lean on.

As the 'teenager' of this suit, the Knight of Pentacles throws themselves into their studies with complete commitment. All of the Knights have a touch of the obsessive about them – here, that is about determined pursuit of a goal. But the Knight of Pentacles is a little wiser than the other Knights – there's an awareness here of the journey ahead, and knowledge that it will take a lot of hard work to get through it.

Still, as a gung-ho teen, this Knight does not have everything figured out. As such, this card can represent directing our focus in the wrong direction, or becoming so lost in the present task we lose sight of the bigger picture or longer term goal. If that speaks to you, press pause for a moment and carefully evaluate your path.

This is the kind of energy we need to draw on when we are in something for the long haul. This is where we learn and practice stamina, where we discover what commitment looks like in practice. It's not always easy, or flashy, or fun. Sometimes it's just about getting our heads down and working on through, one step at a time.

Special skills

Dedication, stamina, hard-working attitude, dependability.

King of Pentacles

A wealthy and generous leader

Here is a person who has achieved great things. Someone wealthy, whether that means materially rich, or simply very comfortable in their own life. This person has all that they need, and they know it, enjoying the feeling of abundance or luxury.

Implicit in this vision of success is a lot of hard work. The King of Pentacles is not someone who has simply happened upon great fortune, but one who has worked for many years. They have been through the many trials of the suit of Pentacles, the ups and the downs. They have been both the Page and the Knight of Pentacles, an eager explorer, and a dedicated worker.

Kings tend to derive power from structures. Their rise to wealth was almost certainly aided by the unequal systems that govern our lives, the different privileges they enjoy having made success and accumulation easier. The King of Pentacles raises questions about the way our economies are structured, and how we as individuals engage with these systems. It asks us to notice the different privileges we all hold (even alongside marginal or oppressed identities), and acknowledge how they benefit our lives and make us more comfortable.

This King values order and common sense, opts for quality over quantity, is careful (though generous) with resources, and has an eye for things that will last. This person may be quite conservative, strongly prizing tradition and structure. In many ways, this card is a lot like the Emperor, concerned with building solid foundations. Whether in our individual lives or in our work in community, this card encourages sensible, sometimes unglamorous decisions that bring long-term returns, saving, rainy-day planning, investments in 'future you' or the future of your community.

In a simpler sense, though, the King of Pentacles card represents a sense of achievement. It may point to a comfortable home, reaching a happy place with your body, a job you love, a well-done community project, or other high points of this earthy suit. This is a time to feel satisfied.

It's also about generosity. When you have this much, what will you do with it? See to your own needs, of course – the King of Pentacles is adept at self-care – but what extra you have, you can share. The King of Pentacles opens their home to people they trust and care about, sharing their resources kindly and with love, and with an eye to the future world they are continually building.

Beyond this, like all Kings, this person may be a leader. Someone who holds a degree of status in society, someone who all can see has 'made it', and who – in the best expression of this card – helps others to do the same. The King of Pentacles asks us to look at how we use this kind of power in our lives – for self-advancement, or for the benefit of wider society?

Special skills

Richness, generosity, leadership.

Queen of Pentacles

Embodying care

This Queen rules the element of earth. Deeply comfortable in their home and environment, the Queen of Pentacles is a nurturing soul, a person who exudes care and compassion. They are the Minor Arcana's embodiment of the Empress archetype.

The Queen of Pentacles is someone who is really grounded in their life. They have learned to feel their way through life, listening to their heart and their body and understanding the way they communicate – on all levels – with their environment. This may be a farmer, a herbalist, a potter, a builder, an artist – anyone who works with physical materials in a magical way, with a deep appreciation of the world's resources, and a respectful, positive way of working with them.

Grounded like this, we experience a feeling of being connected to something far bigger than ourselves. True, the Queen of Pentacles, like the King, may simply indicate a rich or powerful person. But whatever their status, this person is wise, because they know themselves to be part of a big, wide world. A profound sense of belonging is core to their richly satisfying life.

Like the Empress, this Queen values the realm of the senses. They enjoy food and good smells, beauty and music, all that is delicious in life. They have a deeply-rooted sense of abundance, they are resourceful and practical, able to meet their own needs. This person is fabulous at self-care and doesn't hesitate to look after their body's needs.

And like the King of Pentacles, this Queen is also generous. Appreciative of the riches that surround her, she is able to share what she has and nurture others. There are those same themes of caring here – of both giving and receiving nurturing love. You may feel a strong desire (or feel a duty) to care for someone or become a parent. Or maybe you just want to throw a dinner party. However this urge may show up, there is encouragement here to enjoy and share what you have.

All of these characteristics are grounded in gratitude. In having a spiritual connection to the world around us. As the 'highest' card in the Pentacles suit, the Queen has worked carefully with the element of earth, integrating it fully into her being.

Special skills

Grounded, embodied, connected, knows how to take care of herself and her community.

Page of Swords

A quest for truth

As with all Pages, this is a card of curiosity. The Page of Swords is an explorer of the mind, of thoughts, ideas, plans. This person will climb a mountain for the sake of seeing the view. They want to know where they are – and more importantly, they want to know why.

The Page of Swords seeks answers. They may be a student, particularly an academic learner, or someone studying books or words. Remember that Swords are the suit of communication. This is also the suit of logic, and this Page likes to figure out what is going on.

Ever hungry for new perspectives, the Page talks to others, asking questions, gathering a range of views. They want to hear it all. As a 'child', a degree of naivety may be present here, as the Page of Swords is like a sponge soaking up everything around them, perhaps neglecting to work out what their own take on things is.

In a diminished sense this card can indicate paying too much attention to gossip and hearsay, but in it's best expression the Page is someone who is using those diverse opinions as a springboard for forming their own. They listen, they work to understand, but ultimately they are learning to form their own world view and, hopefully, to express it. The Page of Swords encourages us to develop the skill of critical thinking, learning to filter the information we receive through our own sense of what is true, what is just. Stay curious and open, but recognise your power to discern.

Sword held high, the Page is grappling with the element of air – it is sharp, heavy and bold. This is a quest for truth and justice, starting with an open, humble beginner's mind.

Special skills

Curiosity, communicative, seeking truth.

Knight of Swords

Know-it-all

The Knight of Swords has all the answers. 'I've got it!' they shout, rushing headlong into the fray to tell everyone the truth. It's a confident, bold, and dynamic card.

The thing is, they may be right, or they may be wrong. The Knight of Swords doesn't always take the time to check. It looks like they're thinking with their mind, but what they're really listening to is ego – 'This is how I need the truth to be. This is me and what I'm fighting for.' There's a heck of a lot of 'I' in those 'truths', and this card can point to a need to unpack some of this, some of this entanglement of your own identity with the 'facts' you wield.

As a teenager, there's a theme of immaturity again. Wielding that sword of truth with a sometimes clumsy determination, the Knight hasn't taken the time to fact-check or think about consequences. They've got an opinion and it's time for everyone to hear it. The impulse is egotistic, but there's also a genuine belief here that they are right and that their campaign is fair and just (a dedicated social justice activist may find themselves embodying this character, even with the best intentions). The Knight of Swords can certainly be self-righteous. There's arrogance, too, of course – there is arrogance in every Knight.

Sometimes this impulsive 'tell it like it is' energy is what a situation needs. Someone to shake things up a little, make a controversial statement or – just maybe – speak an important and genuine truth. The Knight of Swords isn't known for being careful, but that doesn't mean they are necessarily wrong. This card encourages boldness, recognising that it is sometimes better to speak and risk making a mistake, than to stay in silence or complicity. There is a freeing spirit of experimentation here, but it must be tempered with an awareness of the weight and impact of our words. The Knight of Swords is anti-perfectionist, but needs to learn about compassion and accountability to ensure they don't do harm.

The Knight of Swords may also be a person with a chip on their shoulder. Maybe you've been nursing a grudge, or running over and over some past hurt in your mind. This person can be bitter, resentful, or obsessive. In Pamela Colman-Smith's version of this card, the Knight gallops from right to left, as if towards the past. There is a theme here of being hung up on past events, choosing to dwell in old hurt rather than move forwards.

Special skills

Not afraid to speak – and act on – the truth as they see it. Bold and decisive. Imperfect.

King of Swords

A just communicator

Here, we meet a person who is steadfastly confident in their beliefs. A profoundly fair person, to the point that there is no space for grey areas between the black and the white, the King of Swords lays down the law.

As with all the Kings, this is a person who has worked long and hard to be in this position. Lengthy studies and tough life experiences have brought her to this position, the King of Swords has been through everything we saw in the suit of Swords and has emerged with strong views rooted in a keen appreciation of justice.

The King of Swords may be an excellent teacher, writer or speaker. Communication is a big theme in the Swords, and at this stage, we see a person who has really mastered those skills. They are not only able to formulate their truths, but to clearly express them.

As a leader, this is also someone who brings great planning skills to the table. They are capable of seeing a goal, and carefully, cleverly plotting out the route towards it. A King of Swords takes the long view, anticipates obstacles, plans for success. There may be no problem that this person can think their way around.

They are also incredibly perceptive and able to cut to the heart of a situation. As the King of Swords, you see not only the symptoms, but the issue itself, the root cause. This King makes an excellent and witty social commentator, never missing the opportunity to point out what's really going on.

In terms of advice, the King of Swords encourages you to be very, very rational. To put aside your feelings and ask yourself what is fair, what is objectively right. Let that be your guide.

Special skills

Powerful communicator and leader, strong sense of justice.

Queen of Swords

Compassionate truth

When I ask people to tell me their favourite tarot card, the Queen of Swords often comes up. Why? Because this is a strong, powerful person who has been through a lot. Many of us relate to this Queen's story – all the heartbreak and the conflict we saw in the Swords suit, all of the processing that accompanied that. We see her as a person of tenacity and courage; she represents getting through it, and coming out stronger (though perhaps a little sadder, too).

What gives the Queen of Swords her power is that she has integrated the lessons she has learned. She has taken each of those heartbreaking experiences and the renewal that came after, and forged them into diamonds. She doesn't shy away from what hurts, she has simply moved forward, bringing her diamonds with her. Remember the person in the boat in the Six of Swords, taking their lessons with them to new lands? Here they are twenty years later, strong, wise, and self-aware.

This is a person who is committed to 'doing the work'. That might be deep, personal shadow work, that might be unravelling privilege, that might mean figuring out how to live a life more in line with their principles. This person knows that in order to live authentically, truthfully, they must do inner work. The Queen of Swords is fully, consciously accountable to herself and to the world, yet always aware that there is more to unravel, more to learn.

In the best of the Swords cards, we see the transformative power of mindfulness, the spiritual practice of observing our own minds without judgement. We are able to bring peace to our lives, to calm a chattering mind, through practice and meditation. The Queen of Swords has mastered this practice.

Like the King, she is logical and uses her sword to cut to the heart of the matter, again, keen to see the truth behind any situation. But there is more compassion here. The Queen of Swords does not need to be staunchly black and white, she does not lay down the law. She knows that there are grey areas, too – and that these can be painful places to dwell. She has been there, too.

Again, communication is a powerful skill. The Queen of Swords is able to articulate some of the most challenging truths of our time – she explains not only the sadness in this world, but where it comes from, the systems of injustice and fear that cause harm. She is a visionary, too, and when she shares her vision for a fairer world, all can understand.

Special skills

Compassionate, strong, has been through a lot and does not flinch at tough truths.

Page of Wands

Curiosity in motion

True to their character as a Page, the Page of Wands is a curious person, eager to go on an adventure. This one has the energy of fire under their seat – they're excitable and energetic.

The Page of Wands can be someone who has just had a brilliant idea and is wondering how to set about it. They hold their idea out in front of them and watch how it shimmers. They feel a burning inside as they feel excited about how things will go.

This is someone who wants to learn all about the element of fire. How it shows up in our lives, how we can use it, what it can be used for. They are experimental, ready to make mistakes. They are prepared to reiterate, tweaking and playing with their ideas, learning as they go. Again, the Page of Wands could be a student, perhaps learning about politics, social affairs, business – anything that takes a lot if initiative and dynamism. Or they could represent anyone who is excited to experiment with an idea they've got brewing.

As Wands are the suit of ideals and principles, this may be a person embarking on a social mission. Maybe they've just started to learn about socialism or feminism, or some other radical way of seeing the world that is grounded in a set of principles – and they're excited to find out more and put these principles into practice.

Because 'action' is a core idea for this Page. Wands are all about doing. Manifesting. Making magic. The Page of Wands is inspired by ideas, but is focused on what they might become.

Special skills

Curious, energetic, bold, inspired.

Knight of Wands

Wild charisma

This Knight is all ego. Bold and brash they storm into the centre of things, ready to show the world how great they are. They have that kind of rakish attractiveness about them, something about how wild they seem.

This can be really fun! It's good to have the Knight of Wands around, they're fun at parties and know how to get the crowd going. It's also good to be around this kind of confidence – the Knight of Wands isn't afraid to take the first step and get things moving, inspiring others to come along too.

A typical Knight, this person hasn't quite got a grip on their own power yet, so it often comes out in these clumsy, over the top ways. This card can represent someone who is all fired up with ideas and the urge to act – but hasn't thought or felt things through yet. They don't have a container for their fire, it's just running wild.

Of course, they may take up a lot of space – big egos do that. The Knight of Wands can be someone who dominates spaces with their need for attention. They can be demanding and loud – not to mention arrogant. This person asserts themselves with confidence – yet at the same time, they need a lot of validation to keep that confidence rolling. There is encouragement in this card to look at the ways we seek validation, and the role of performativity in our lives, so we can draw ourselves back towards truth and authenticity.

This is an inspiring person who loves to lead – maybe someone in your peer group who seems to have a really fun, adventurous life or someone you'd like to be around. Their energy is infectious and people are drawn to their easy charisma.

Special powers

Dynamic, bold, fiery, attractive to others.

King of Wands

Confident leadership

Where the Knight of Wands showed us untamed dynamism, the King is the real deal. This is someone who gets things done. Fuelled by inspiration, they have the wisdom and experience to actually bring ideas into the real world. They see things through, and this is a card for completion and achievement.

All Kings are leaders, and the King of Wands is the leader who inspires others. We trust that this person is not 'all talk', but will follow through on their promises. There's follow-through. There's that charisma again, this time it's grounded and sexy in its steadiness. Other people just want to be around this energy, lap up the King's ideas, feel secure in their leadership.

Having reached this position, this person may be great at delegating. They have worked their way through the many trials of the wands suit and knows how to discern between activities that are actually worth time and energy, and tasks that can be dropped or handed over. They don't need to micromanage, because they know that they are in control.

The arrogance we see in the Knight has mellowed into a deep sense of self-confidence. The King, having been both Page and Knight, has failed many times in the past and knows how to approach projects calmly, with all that fire carefully controlled and poised. There's no need to rush headlong into things – this King is bold and considered, strong rather than wild. Channelling that archetypal Magician energy, the King of Wands is at all times connected to and acting from their intention. Rather than their ego directing their fire, it is intention, values and passion that steers.

Special skills

Confident, natural group leader, sees things through, charismatic, intentional.

Queen of Wands

Creative confidence

This is the kind of person everybody wants to be. The Queen of Wands has all the confidence and dynamism of the other Wands characters, but hers is truly grounded in passion. She lives a life that she really loves, and owns it all with joy (even the rocky patches – this isn't about having a 'perfect life').

This is not only a person who gets things done, but who is creative. In art, in business, in life, in any sphere, the Queen of Wands does things her way – she learned a long time ago not to compromise herself or fit herself to others' moulds. Onlookers may view her with mixed opinions – some loving her daring, colourful style, some disapproving. Nobody could say that she was living any life but her own.

This may be an unusual person, someone who does things differently, but there's no fear or shame in it. The Queen of Wands is loud and proud, and never apologises for herself. Like all Queens, she has 'done the work', she's looked deeply into her own soul, she has understood on a spiritual level who she is. Knowing this, she doesn't care about anyone else's opinion. She's doing great as she is.

Not that she is without compassion. Charismatic like the King, the Queen of Wands may have many friends or be sociable and outgoing. (It's also possible that she might be an introvert – despite her confidence.) But she's also a good friend who shows up when you need her. As a leader, she knows how to play to everyone's strengths and make folks feel good.

This Queen represents having a true passion for your work, for being inspired and working on projects, feeling really in tune with what you're doing. The Queen of Wands can be quick and energetic, there is an exciting feeling of creative opportunities, diverse possibilities. Like the King, she inspires with a grounded 'yes' energy.

The most important characteristic of the Queen of Wands is her lust for life. This is a positive person who feels abundant. If there is something she needs that she doesn't have, she manifests it through sheer force of will – she believes in good things, asks for them, and expects them. All Queens are witches, and this person works with the fiery energy of the Universe, tapping into bigger forces to make her desires come to life.

Special skills

Lust for life, self-belief, completely unbothered by others' opinions.

Page of Cups

The heart's adventure

This Page's curiosity is directed to all things heart- and soul-centred. The Page of Cups is eager to fall in love, ready to hand her heart over, overflowing with the willingness to open up and share.

It's a beautiful, happy, innocent card, representing a person who acts like they've never been hurt. They can feel their heart beating and want to take it — or follow it — on a journey. In some cards, we see the image of a fish leaping out of a cup. The fish represents spirituality and reminds us that this will be a spiritual journey, but the Page's attitude is one of playfulness. They see the beauty in this, but also the fun. They hold their spirituality lightly.

This needn't be about love or romance – the Page of Cups is an explorer of the soul, too. Theirs is the realm of water; intuition, and magic, as well as feelings and emotions. They may not fully understand what is meant by 'follow your bliss', but they know that's what they want to do. This card could point to experimenting with different spiritual or religious practices, exploring different ways of understanding or expressing their spirituality. This is a good time to try something new, perhaps something you've been cynical about in the past, or something that has always called to you.

Enter into this journey with a lightness of heart and an expectation that it will be enjoyable. Don't take things too seriously at this moment. Journeys of the soul can indeed be challenging, there may be dark times on the path, but this is about going in with an eagerness, a curiosity, a light sprit, and a readiness for adventure.

Special skills

Open-hearted, honest, lightness and non-attachment, eager to explore emotions and spirituality.

Knight of Cups

Feeling without form

Unlike the Page, the Knight of Cups is taking their journey very seriously indeed. It may even be all they do, as they are consumed by this experience of following their heart and soul. In many ways, this card represents falling in love, in that the Knight is utterly enthralled by the ebb and flow of her own heart. It can be a beautiful experience, but it can also represent becoming emotionally stuck. I always find it interesting how it seems the more seriously we take ourselves, the less accessible enlightenment becomes. The Page of Cups, with her lightness of spirit, seems far more likely to discover great truths than this Knight, brooding and serious.

This person may have become lost in their journey. Obsessive love is one expression of the Knight of Cups, as is a person who has become overly attached to self-help books or spiritual doctrine. It's possible to go so far into these deep and fascinating explorations that we lose track of our own lived reality. This Knight is often brooding, moody, at the mercy of their heart's fluctuations. They feel everything ten times over, ten times as strong.

> *I went to the doctor, I went to the mountains*
> *I looked to the children, I drank from the fountains*
> *There's more than one answer to these questions*
> *Pointing me in a crooked line*
> *And the less I seek my source for some definitive*

Indigo Girls, *'Closer to Fine'*

Despite the strength of feeling, there's a passivity here. Where the Knight of Pentacles' dedication leads her slowly towards a goal, the Knight of Cups stands still. It's an impasse. In order to really move forwards, that emotion needs shape. The Knight of Cups is like water without a container – all that deep feeling is swirling, but has no form, no real expression. And without form it is in danger of becoming superficial, even meaningless.

But this card can also represent a person who is just taking the time to immerse themselves in pure feeling. It is not always necessary to find containers for or 'give shape' to our emotions, or articulate our spiritual journeys. The Knight of Cups can represent a person who has allowed themselves to surrender – and that can be a beautiful thing. Remember that Knights represent extremes, and know that this is a short-term situation – to remain in this place too long risks becoming stuck or lost, but it is good to allow ourselves space to sink into pure feeling.

This card can simply point to a person who is falling in love or who is being very romantic. There is a fun element to the Knight of Cups, too – they may just be encouraging you to buy a bunch of roses for someone you love.

Special skills

Surrender, deeply romantic.

King of Cups

Controlled emotion

Kings achieve their power through experience, lineage and structure. The King of Cups is someone who has seen a lot in their life, experienced many trials of the heart, and is now 'in control'. They've 'done the work' and feel they have achieved a position of stability and strength.

They may keep a close rein on their feelings – the King of Cups is a person who does not seem open-hearted, and who doesn't like to feel vulnerable. They tend to give the impression of being emotionally 'sorted' and are not easily swayed in emotional matters. In the most harmful expression of this King, this may represent a person who has built up too-rigid boundaries around their heart. In their efforts to stay in control they have become cut-off. It can be hard to know what the King of Cups is really feeling because they maintain this tight control and do not give much away.

This card can also represent the overthinking part of our emotional lives. It's easy to become caught in self-development and spiritual theory and tools (especially if we've been through a hard time and have sought help with processing), but in doing so we risk mistaking intellectual learning for doing the work itself. The work, of course, being feeling. In a positive light, the King of Cups represents the ability not just to learn, but to apply self-help and spiritual learnings to our own lives, to turn theory into lived practice.

The King of Cups may also be someone who holds a position of authority in spiritual or emotional affairs. They may be a psychologist or a therapist, or a spiritual leader of some sort. A very positive expression of this King would be a person who, drawing on their studies and their own life experience, assists other people to achieve spiritual balance. Along with experience and study has come the ability to look deeper into matters of the heart and soul, and they are able to analyse and articulate what is going on for troubled people, as for themselves.

Special skills

Emotionally 'sorted' (or at least appearing so), psychoanalytical, a 'rock' in hard times.

Queen of Cups

Emotional freedom

Here is a person who has done a lot (*a lot*) of deep spiritual work and has integrated their lessons fully. They know who they are, they know how to listen to their heart, how to make heart-centred decisions and live an authentic, spiritually nourishing life.

Like the King, the Queen of Cups has had plenty of experience in matters of the heart. They have searched and experimented, moved through break-ups and new love, given and received and lost in friendship, learned about kindness and compassion and grief. They may be a person who helps others in their own journeys; a therapist, a mentor, a listener.

This is an intuitive person, someone who needs to feel a thing in order to know it. Empathetic, they can 'tune in' to the people they meet and understand them on a deep level. This can make some folks feel uneasy around the Queen of Cups, whilst others may feel a sense of ease at being witnessed so fully. This is someone who tends to see people for who they are, without judgement.

They gift this same care and compassion to themselves. Ultimately these external, visible qualities emanate from a profound inner place. The Queen of Cups knows himself. He knows, like the Queen of Pentacles, how deeply he is connected to the whole Universe, and is grounded in his emotional life, well practiced in feeling his way through. He draws on embodied practices to help him stay in alignment with his desires, his longing. It may not always be steady, but he owns his life with passion. He knows how to listen. He knows how to tune out the noise and hear what his heart has to say in any situation. This card encourages you to draw on that power and listen deep.

Any 'witchy' practice can be associated with the Queen of Cups: spellwork, magic, lunar love, tarot and astrology, goddess-work, ritual. She gathers her tools with intention, ensuring she is equipped to delve deeper into her practice and explore further, or try new things.

Special skills

Empathetic, deeply intuitive and honest, creative, ability to sit with difficult feelings and hold space for others to do the same.

Tarot Spreads

A tarot spread is a specific layout of cards, where each position has its own meaning. Moving beyond the one-card reading (which is a spread in its own right), spreads are how we carry out tarot readings.

You can refer back to the earlier sections on this book on Tarot for Self-Care and Creating a Daily Practice for ideas and guidance around preparing for a reading.

To use one of these spreads, shuffle the cards in your preferred way. Then lay them out as shown in the picture. You may lay your cards face down, turning them over one by one as you work through the reading. Or you may lay them face up. You may find that cards you lay are upside down – it is up to you whether you leave them this way, or read them 'reversed' (see the next section).

If you've laid your cards face up, before delving into the reading, try to take in first impressions of the whole thing. Does any specific image or symbol jump out at you? Is there symmetry between the cards, or other kinds of patterns you can see? Can you describe how you feel, on looking at this reading as a whole?

When you are ready, begin to interpret the cards individually. Read the card position, then interpret this card in that position (for example, read the card as 'the heart of the issue', or 'a direction to head in'.) Refer back to the card interpretations given in this book any time you like, but leave room for your own ideas to come through.

When you've read each card, come back to the big picture, the spread as a whole. What story have the cards told you? What key themes have emerged? Does the whole reading have a message you can summarise? How do you feel about this reading now?

Two-Card Cross

This short and sweet tarot reading helps to break through confusion, offering a snapshot of our current situation, then a word of advice to move us forwards or help us frame our situation usefully.

Card positions:

1. Current situation. How does this card reflect what's going on for you right now, or what aspect of your situation is calling for your attention?

2. Advice or guidance.

Three-Card Spread

This simple spread places one leading card in the centre, then offers two further 'supporting' cards that offer a deeper interpretation of the first.

Card positions:

1. Central card, the heart of the issue.

2 & 3. Context, guidance, further information.

The Bridge

This is my most used tarot spread. It places the seeker at the apex of a bridge –
the present moment. From this vantage point we are able to look back across
the journey so far, then forward to next steps. Additional cards offer guidance.

Card positions:

1. You, the situation, the present moment.

2. The past, where you started from, something you've left or are leaving
behind.

3. A lesson learned along the way, or how you've grown.

4. The river: unconscious influences, possibly unseen.

5. Next steps, what to do or focus on now.

6. Overall direction to head in.

7. Guiding star: a word of guidance or advice.

The Celtic Cross

The Celtic Cross is a large, wide-ranging spread that can be used to tackle nearly any query. It offers an overview of our current situation, with a variety of perspectives that help us see our experiences in different lights.

This classic spread has many iterations. This one is mine, but you may encounter many variations on your travels.

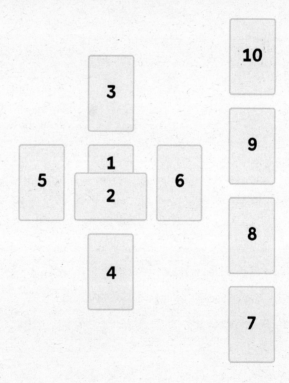

Card positions:

1. The centre of the situation.

2. 'Crossing' card – something which is blocking the situation and providing a challenge to be overcome.

3. Above – what you are consciously manifesting or outwardly presenting.

4. Below – what is underlying the situation, which you may or may not be aware of.

5. Passing – an energy which has been significant in bringing you to this point, but which is now leaving (or has left) your life.

6. Coming in – energy which is now entering your life and is playing a significant role in moving things forwards (whether for better or worse).

7. You, now – where you're at, how you're feeling, this card represents you.

8. External influences – something that is impacting on the situation which comes from outside of you. This could be a person, a system, an energy or a situation you have no control over.

9. Hopes and fears – it's surprising how the same thing can be both a hope and a fear! This card represents the thing you long for, yet also want to avoid ...

10. Outcome – traditionally, this is the 'outcome' or 'outcome if nothing changes' card. Feel free to rename this card as per the 'predictive tarot and outcome cards' exercise in this chapter! I like to call this the 'advice' card.

Lineage and Resources

Nothing in this book would have come to exist if I did not belong to a rich, diverse, wonderful community of tarot readers and writers, activists, witches, thinkers, feelers, teachers and guides.

In setting out my own guidance for journeying with the tarot, I draw on a long, wide lineage of tarot lovers who came before me and alongside me. Everything I know about tarot was teased out and given shape by books, teachers, deck creators, bloggers, friends, and others who have guided me deeper into my cards.

My first tarot books were both by queer women (Rachel Pollack and Barbara Moore), and my personal tarot lineage is one rooted in queer culture and decolonisation of body, mind and soul. It is impossible to name and thank everyone I have been influenced by, or to count the many ways I've been guided by queer and trans folx, Black people and people of colour. I can only offer my deepest gratitude to everyone out there who works to diversify, explore, and make more accessible the world of tarot. I'm thrilled that you exist and that you do what you do. I love you, and I am beyond grateful for all that you offer.

That said, I'd love to name just a few of my faves from the queer tarot family:

- Alexis J Cunningfolk. Alexis, who runs the Worts + Cunning apothecary, blog and school, is one of those unicorn people who can teach us - by showing us - how to truly integrate our spiritual, political and material lives. Their teachings on plants and folklore, tarot, astrology and self-care have inspired my personal practice for years. Explore Alexis' work at wortsandcunning.com

- Cathou. Where to begin with colourful, beautiful Cathou? A self-described artivist and fat femme, her Instagram is both a gorgeous celebration of self-love and a discussion space for radical, political spiritual practice. Follow along at instagram.com/cathoutarot

- Asali. Earthworker, magical tea-blender, tarot reader and writer Asali is the creator of the Tarot of the QTPOC project, which has been an invaluable resource for many in our community for years. Her writings, rooted in queer, Black and femme identities, were some of the most potent and beautiful pieces published on the LRT community blog. Find her at asaliearthwork.com

- Rebekah Erev. It is hard for me to think of another soul who pours as much love into the witchy queer community as artist and Hebrew priestess Rebekah. I feel comforted simply knowing she is in this world, and her unique Malakh Halevanah oracle deck is a tool I turn to for comfort and inspiration regularly. Find her at rebekaherevstudio.com

- Sarah Gottesdiener. Moon-witch Sarah gifts us a beautiful, ever-unfolding lunar map via her monthly Moonbeaming newsletter. She's also the creator of the Many Moons Planner - an incredible annual project that brings together radical and wise voices from many corners of our communities. Find Sarah at visualmagic.info

There are more, many more. Cassandra Snow, Cedar McCloud, Siobhan Rene,

Andi Grace and Abbie Plouff have all impacted my relationship with tarot, along with countless others. And though I'm no astrologer, I'm joyfully swayed by queer astrologers Alice Sparkly Kat, Corina Dross, and Chani Nicholas, whose work positions astrology as another liberatory tool.

In terms of tarot guidebooks, my favourites include *She Is Sitting in the Night: Revisioning Thea's Tarot* by Oliver Pickle, *Modern Tarot* by Michelle Tea, and of course *Seventy-Eight Degrees of Wisdom* by Rachel Pollack.

As I write this in 2020, in the midst of a global pandemic, I am finding it particularly difficult to focus on written words. I am grateful for the existence of podcasts such as Sarah Cargill's *Tarot for the End of Times*, which journeys through the cards one by one exploring, as their name suggests, their relationship to this era of intense change and the opportunity for revolution embedded within. I highly recommend tuning in.

Lastly, social justice activist, facilitator, doula and author adrienne maree brown warrants a special shoutout for her huge influence on my thinking and practice. I've lost count of the ways amb's earth-shifting work has returned me, over and over, to the question of 'what am I practicing?' Each time I sit with this simple yet profound enquiry, I deepen my connection to what I love, and new possibilities unfold. Though primarily a tool for activists, I recommend amb's groundbreaking book *Emergent Strategy* to all who wish to marry their tarot and spiritual practice to practices of liberation, justice, collaboration, and care. This book is referenced just a couple of times in this book, but amb's teachings are less visibly present throughout, and increasingly inform my approach to tarot. Find adrienne's writing and more at adriennemareebrown.net

The Little Red Tarot Community Blog

The LRT community blog is a digital coffee-table book, an archive of seven years of writing from across our beautiful, diverse community. Beginning as my personal blog many years ago, writers of many backgrounds came together on this site to create a haven and a hub for alternative, queered, decolonised, self-care rooted, liberation centred perspectives on the tarot and much more.

You can explore all of this at blog.littleredtarot.com

About Beth

Beth Maiden is the founder of Little Red Tarot, a social enterprise shop and resource for lovers of independently-published tarot and oracle decks, books and tools for radical magic. She is the creator of the popular, long-running Alternative Tarot Course, and the author of many long and rambling blog posts telling her own life story through the cards.

Beth lives in rural Wales with her partner and cats. She loves photography, music, dancing and long walks. Her favourite deck is Thea's Tarot, by Ruth West.

Find Beth's work online:

Little Red Tarot	littleredtarot.com
The Alternative Tarot Course	littleredtarot.com/atc
LRT Community blog archive	blog.littleredtarot.com
Beth's personal website	bethmaiden.com